PAGE PUBLISHING

POETRY ANTHOLOGY

VOLUME 5

Donnie Pike
Yvonne Hewitt
Lorrie West
Tom Decarme
Reggie Harris
Toni Burgess
Leonard London Jr.
Tamara Deanne Hawkins
Betty Winkler
Musa Lang

PAGE PUBLISHING, INC.
New York, NY

First originally published by Page Publishing, Inc. 2019

ISBN 978-1-64462-068-7 (Paperback)
ISBN 978-1-64462-069-4 (Digital)

Printed in the United States of America

CONTENTS

Donnie Pike 5

Yvonne Hewitt 49

Lorrie West...61

Tom Decarme 69

Reggie Harris 81

Toni Burgess...117

Leonard London Jr. 163

Tamara Deanne Hawkins 197

Betty Winkler...223

Musa Lang 245

A Poet's Journey

DONNIE PIKE

A Journey to Heaven

If I stay up late thinking about this day,
Counting sheep, losing sleep & what is the meaning of life,
The only thing I gain is the loss of sleep.
Sometimes the Wind Blows.
I can feel them.
I can't see them,
But I can hear them too.
Often times I think about the Journey to Heaven & what Heaven is like.
This time I don't mind losing sleep.
Sometimes the Wind blows, and I can hear the voice of Angels whispering to me softly telling me,
"It's Beautiful Here"
Sometimes I sleep and sometimes I dream.
Sometimes I don't lose sleep thinking about the Journey.
Because sometimes the wind blows, and I can hear you & I can feel you too.
Sometimes I don't mind losing sleep.
Sometimes the Wind Blows,
Sometimes I dream about,
The Journey to Heaven.

Last Days

Journeys with no end, is that possible?

As you have memories of days gone by,
Thoughts enter your mind that we are living in our last days,

I wonder, is this true?

As Christians we believe in the Holy Spirit,
King of Kings, the Almighty God,
Power over all things, good & evil.

Knowing this as Christians,
We also know that everyday life is a struggle,
A struggle to keep the faith in knowing,

~God Has Got This~

Our Last Days…?
I believe we are living in the days of new beginnings.
I believe the last days belong to Satan,
These are the last days of the devil.

As we dance in delight,
We celebrate as born-again Christians in the family of the Holy Spirit.

We take each day as a challenge,
Each day as a new experience,
A tool to carry us through the trials of everyday life.

As children in the family of God,
We teach His Word along our journey in this hour glass of life.
We will lift them up when they fall.
We give them a shoulder to cry on,

And then we say to them…

~GOD HAS GOT THIS~

And then we journey on,
Knowing.

The last days are not a burden for us to bear,
But yet new beginnings for us to share…

Barefoot in the Snow

Temporarily insane but never lost he wouldn't be back until he cap-
tured his dreams,
A reflection of himself lay in shadows like the shoes he left at the fork
in the road.
Running into nowhere trying to save time in the company of strang-
ers he stands alone making notes in his mind that will never be
read.
Declaring himself as a Gypsy Traveler with his heart in his hand he
wouldn't be seeking Refuge,

He Cried Out to His Soul.

The cost of freedom is losing yourself before you can find it,
Being swallowed by Mother Nature is the first payment.
The first step of Awakening would be the hardest,
Standing before a Mountain of dreams not letting the past remind
him of what he is now,
Like sliding downhill with people in the way, what have you got to
lose if you let go?

The little voice inside is no longer speaking,
Who then can be lonely if you find yourself?
He held his breath and took another step.
Touch the Sparrow, hide the Sun with the Moon.

Being powerless by his own Manifestation the Weary Traveler walks
Barefoot in the Snow…

The Whispering Mountains

By the light of the moon she lies in silence like a porcelain image
   pondering the stars,
Meditating on her faerie forest that lives inside the quiet wilderness
   gone frozen in time.

As I gaze at this majestic giant, the whispering mountains speak vol-
   umes into my heart & fill my soul with peace.
I am in awe of such beauty that has the power to change the course of
   a flowing river, but instead lives in harmony with it.

The sky above whispers songs in passing the relaxing meadows that
   lie on top of this vast landscape that is in perfect view of a blue
   horizon.
As I plant a seed in the garden of my mind, I am swept away by this
   place & only in my mind can I hear,

The Whispering Mountains…

Battling the Storm

An unpredictable life can leave you lost at sea Battling the Storm,

There will always be storms to fight, seas to cross & journeys that seem to never end.

The survivors of life's voyage will be the ones that never give up.

The ones that remain focused & guided their ship through the storm.

There is a calming beauty after a storm, the same in life.

The survivors of life's journey reap the rewards & leave behind a legacy for others to follow.

Remember, the hourglass of time leads to a peaceful journey,

But only if you are willing to make the necessary sacrifices.

Only then will you find your rainbow.

Seven Doves to Heaven

Every beginning has an ending, and every ending has a new beginning.

Our journey through life teaches us to look for the signs.

Moonlit nights and sounds of silence hold the secrets to an untold story,

About to be read through your life.

Your journey began when you were falling into flight.

The first time I saw it I was praying, asking God for a sign,

He sent me a dove.

I sang songs of gratitude.

The next time I saw it the hand of God touched my father,

It was the touch of Grace.

I asked God "Why? Give me a sign", he sent me two doves,

~I found Grace~

The next time I saw it another soul entered the kingdom of Heaven,

I prayed and asked God to give me Peace,

He sent me three more,

~I found Peace~

The passing of time has a healing breeze,

It comes in the form of the wings of a dove in flight.

As one falls into flight, another one takes its place.

Journey's end and new Journeys begin,

Seven Doves to Heaven…

Arise

As you wake each day, to face an uncertain world that constantly tries to bury your soul alive with the meaningless complaints about the way you live your life,

You Arise like a Warrior from a grave.

Your only weapons are the knowledge you've gained on your journey through this unstable environment. The knowledge is a sword that strikes fear into the very heart of those that try to control your destiny.

You continue your journey with this knowledge, fully aware that no one can contain the wisdom nor the human spirit that lives inside of you,

And being buried alive each day is a mere fraction that only slows you down enough to rest your body & soul.

Your fight begins now so Arise…

Decompress

Decompress, a mental rebuilding state of mind,

A way to reflect when the world seems so unkind.

Close your eyes & open your mind,

A place of refuge in your soul you will find.

Breathe deep & fill your spirit.

Relaxing music, can you hear it?

On angel's wings your thoughts take flight,

Beyond the horizon, towards the Heavenly light.

Guided by Heaven's angels above,

The power of God & His Unconditional Love.

Set free from problems, give God your stress,

Breathe deep & decompress.

The Invisible Mailbox

Letters that I've written & stories that I've told, are stored in my mind & never grow old.

Destinations to places & people unseen, visions in my mind like a magical dream.

The bones in my hand as I begin to write, a darkened room in the middle of the night.

My mind is on fire, & fire is light.

Whispers of memories in the silent night.

A Silhouette of Love

The first time I saw her she was across the room,
All I could see was her eyes.
As I fantasized about her, I could smell her body,
I knew how her lips would taste,
I could feel her breath against my ear.
As I moved closer across the room our eyes never lost sight of each
     other,
Our minds were as one,
She knew what I wanted,
I hoped she wanted the same thing.
As the crowd moved aside,
It was like a silhouette in motion of passion & emotion meeting for
     the first time.
As we grew closer to each other, the silence of the room was deafening,
To the point the only sound was that of two hearts beating.
Just before the fantasy became reality,
She turned and started to walk away.
And as I lunged toward her, I grabbed her like someone falling from
     a ledge,
I swung her toward me & took control of her lips,
She pretended she was not thinking the same thing I was,
But I knew she was,
Her voice said no, but her breath said yes!
As we shared our first kiss it was like nothing I had ever experienced
     before,
It was more than just a kiss,
It was like a breath of fresh air,
It was like a cool summer rain after a hot day,
It was the beginning of something beautiful,
It was the start of a journey that I hoped would never end.
As we stopped briefly to stare into each other's eyes,
I could tell by the look on her face that she had the same vision as I did,
The vision of a journey with no end filled with all the things that life
     had to offer.

As I stared deeper into her eyes,
I could feel her soul reaching out to mine as if to say,
"The only ones on this journey would be you & I together.
We would soar to the Heavens and touch the Hand of God.
And He would guide the two of us to the edge of Heaven,
Only to realize the Heaven we know is the Heaven we share when
     we are together.
There is no other place I would rather be than by your side."

The Castle

As I gazed across the land the castle came into view,
I wasn't sure what I would find there, but my journey led me to this
      place.
Perhaps I had found Paradise?

With each step I grew closer,
And then, I saw her face.
As she stared out across the horizon, thoughts in my mind begging
      to escape.

What was she searching for?
What had this beautiful creature been waiting on?

Perhaps this very moment in time.
Was it me her soul was searching for?

If time would tell perhaps the time was now.
As time stood still for that very moment, my journey was end.
And ours had just begun…

A Journey of a New Path

Quietly the mind speaks to the heart,
Surrounded by silence the Soul breaks through the madness trapped
inside the human body,
Searching for an escape from the unforgiving world,
That tries to ambush the thrill seeker by obtaining the clear con-
science of a man searching for peace.
A Beast that lives without question trapped inside the human body
will eventually break free,
And conquer & destroy that which tries to defeat them & control
them in an uncontrolled environment.
Who then sacrifices themselves to take back what has been taken?
A man that asks for nothing in return can only take so much from a
world that continually asks for more than its fair share.
The next step is oftentimes bigger then the last,
But is required in order to continue the Journey that goes far beyond
the world's expectations of someone on,
A Journey of a New Path

Faith Brought Me Home

~ "Whoever believes in me may come and drink. For the Scriptures declare rivers of living water will flow from his heart" John 7:38 ~

If I journey to the edge of my mind,
The last image I find is the one that releases my soul.
I find myself not at the end of my journey,
Yet at the beginning.
As the awakening from my promise keeper begins,
I see myself standing between Heaven and Earth like a Gateway.
I can only imagine what the next image will be,
Standing before the Mountain of God.
On bended knee I will rise and touch the hand of an Angel that leads
    me to that mountain,
Like a mermaid from the sea the vision comes to me,
Escaping the world and landing on a beach in Heaven.
No more shadows from a disappointed sky,
My sins left behind as I feel a silent breeze,
I smell the aroma of a Rose,
I accept the light that surrounds me.
The Warrior Ways are laid to rest,
I realize that tomorrow; 'Is Promised' & the dreams of paradise no
    longer live in my head,
They come to life where prayers are read.
The drops of rain return to Heaven & taste like candy not like tears,
The dawn of a new day begins on a simple man's journey,
And it is at that time that I realize it was faith that brought me here,
It was Faith that Brought Me Home…

Time Untie My Hands

If I could go back in time, I would take you with me & watch the
world through the sands of time.

If I could see into tomorrow, I would reach for the stars & give you
the moon.

But I need 'time, to untie my hands'.

If I could change the bad things that 'were' to the good things that
'are' I would give you a perfect world.

But I need 'time, to untie my hands'.

If I could lead you to Heaven's Gate and back again I would do it for
you on good days & bad.

But I need 'time, to untie my hands'.

If I could stop time to stare into your eyes, tomorrow would never
come.

But I need 'time, to untie my hands'.

If I could change one second into one hour, & one hour into one
day, & one day into eternity, I would do it to spend all of my
time with you.

But I need 'time, to untie my hands'.

If I could promise you, we will grow old together because the foun-
tain of youth lives in our hearts and pumps through our veins,
I would keep my word.

But I need 'time, to untie my hands'.

I will spend all of my days with you, my heart is yours, part of my
soul lives in you.

My arms hold you close to me until 'time, unties my hands'.

Without Boundaries

The ones that have boundaries are missing out on the best part of life.

Have you ever just stood by a river and studied it?
The shape, the flow,
The way the water rushes over the boulders?
It's quite beautiful.

But you see,
The river doesn't ask for permission,
The river wasn't afraid of offending the boulder,
The boulder 'takes it' from the river on a daily basis without complaint.
The river is different & makes no apologies for itself.

And the best part of all?

The river is unique & beautiful in its own way for what it is,
Just as the boulder is unique & beautiful in its very own special way.

We all need to be more like the river & keep on flowing & changing & make no apologies for being who we are.

The bottom line is this,

We were created by God & nothing or nobody can change that.
Be who you are for yourself & for God.
That's how you teach the world to Love,

~Without Boundaries~

Answers to Life's Questions

Sometimes the world is a bit too demanding,
Oftentimes we find ourselves drowning in our own self-pity,
Looking for excuses that don't really exist.
How do we keep ourselves from feeling this self-pity?
That's like asking the beautiful sunrise how it can rise when the world
    is such an ugly place,
How can the sunset take your breath away when there is so much
    ugliness in the world?
Sometimes we find ourselves asking the world to stop so we can get
    off,
We say to God, "this is too much for me to handle, I want off."
You can tell yourself, ask God for the answers but sometimes God
    wants you to find the answers to life's questions on your own.
How do you find the answers to the questions when you're not sure
    what the quiz is about?
Is self-pity a way of getting off and starting again?
And what if you get off for that one brief moment, are you then
    going to ask yourself, "What did I miss?"
Did I miss something while I was drowning in my own sorrows try-
    ing to figure out what the meaning of life was all about?
None of us have the right answers,
All we have is the hope for a new day,
Maybe there are no right answers & the questions we have are just
    meaningless overviews of something that doesn't need to be
    reviewed in the first place.
What then?
Sometimes we just need to breathe,
We just need to appreciate that beautiful sunrise,
Stare into that sunset
Give thanks to God for this day & ourselves for hanging on when the
    test was so confusing.

Perhaps that is the answer?
Maybe the only answer is not about life at all,
Maybe the answer is that you just lived, loved & gave a part of yourself
to try & convince the world it's not that bad of a place after all?

Encounter God

A chance encounter with God,

Confusion is nothing new with a suitcase filled with dreams and desires searching for a rainbow,

Chasing the moonlight into darkness on a path of destruction and touching the sounds of silence,

Trying to carry the world on your shoulders.

Scattered stones need guidance, a path makes its own.

Take my hand that I reach out to you, if you fall, I will catch you and you will fly,

God the shelter from the storm.

Rejoice in the dance of salvation, drink in the spirit of love, taste the wine of peace.

Spread your eternal wings and fly into the arms of the Lord on your journey to

Encounter God…

Reckless

The whispering songs played out a silent melody in his mind that set
   his soul on fire yearning for a place to be free,
A journey to find peace.
It was man and machine on a road filled with diamonds,
A long stretch of highway,
Chasing the sunset as it lit up the sky like fireflies that dance around
   a campfire in the misty mountains under the stars in the quiet
   darkness.
His Reckless Dreams that once seemed to be lost in his own mind
   suddenly come to life,
Like the machine that would alter the course on a desolate road with
   no direction home.
Long May He Run,
Reckless…

A Place to Lay

We planted a garden in a place to stay, He dug a hole for a place to lay.

We planted grass around the waterfall and pool, He dug a hole because it was cool.

We built a wall with cement & rock so it would stay, He dug a hole for a place to lay.

We planted a tree for an anniversary we shared, He dug a hole and laid there & stared.

We put up a fence so he could run and play, He dug a hole so he would have a place to lay.

We tied him to a pole under the shadiest tree, He broke the chain because he wanted to be free.

We love him so we gave him the yard, He dug a hole so he can lay there and guard.

We gave him our hearts because he was so true, He dug a hole and now he lays there too...

Winter

Winter,

A dismal may of frozen images stalking the quiet whispers of Mother Nature.

A darkened gloom of a shadowy haze in the bitter cold of a frozen tundra in the middle of a Siberian landscape.

A cosmic ray of glittering ice that freezes the breath of anything that dares to challenge the unforgiving harsh cold of Old Man Winter.

Winter,

A distant memory that re-introduces itself with a vengeance of constructed beauty under the guidance of Mother Nature.

A timeless mosaic dance composed by itself that's time is short lived but never forgotten.

Winter.

Free My Soul

I walked a million miles in my mind searching for the missing piece.

On bended knee I cried a river trying to come to grips with something that wasn't there,

Not realizing my journey has only begun.

The steps I left behind were no longer visible,

Which led me to the conclusion that going back would result in being lost & confused.

Going back is not an option; so, I followed the sunset.

Pride & perseverance drove me on.

Whatever tomorrow brings, I'll be there searching for that missing piece,

One step at a time, one more mountain to climb, another sunset to chase.

Every new goal reached is a victory,

Every new goal set is another missing piece,

Every new day is the beginning of a new journey.

As the voyage continues, I realize the Journey is the missing piece,

And what I am searching for is that place to,

Free my Soul…

The Silent Walls

Beneath the clouds in a midnight grey, the body lies quietly like molded clay.

A vision of earth below the sky, mindscapes of nature captured in the eye.

The peaceful sounds of ocean waves or sounds of cries like tortured slaves.

A subtle breeze on flowing hair, or whistling winds across trees that stare.

Scattered stones lay on the beach, like long lost love that is out of reach.

Like a broken heart afraid to be found, a cry for love but there is no sound.

A grasp in time that has no reason, a peaceful moment like the change of a season.

The echoing sounds of rain that falls, empty inside the silent walls...

A Prisoner of Love

Broken hearts carry dreams that no longer matter,

When love is lost the heart gets shattered.

Slow lonely walks with time & emotion,

You give your heart with total devotion.

Through troubled waters I carry my heart on my sleeve,

My heart found love, why did it leave?

Sleepless nights & days with no light,

A broken heart with no will to fight.

Curious thoughts at what lies ahead,

Memories of love & words that were said, are tattooed on my heart & stored in my head.

Bitter thoughts of how much was real,

I gave you my heart, but it was never yours to steal.

Darkness returns with the stars above,

With every dream I am,

A Prisoner of Love.

The Moon in the Clouds

A light from Heaven shines through the night, just like me God stays up late to write.

Words of love and do not hate, words of wisdom that are not too late.

Words of stories where families win, His unconditional love and forgiven sin.

Beautiful stories written in the sky, some make you rejoice, some make you cry.

Some take you to a place where you can fly, stories that make it easier to say goodbye.

God the Poet from Heaven above, His beautiful words are filled with love.

The words He writes are of triumph and sacrifice, if you did it wrong, don't do it twice.

The Holy Spirit is a Father so proud, He stays up late to write;

By the Moon in the Clouds.

The Crooked Bridge

The hands of light from within, a journey through time where life begins.

Shadowscapes on forest floors, new beginnings and open doors.

Uncharted paths with no footsteps ahead, a whisper in time where no words were said.

A brush with death near a journeys end, a peaceful moment like a new best friend.
Time is short and the voyage is long, nature's melody like a beautiful song.

A magical place inside your head, like a guardian Angel watching over your bed.

Flowers in the garden and birds in the tree, a moment of peace a soul that is free.

A narrow road that lies ahead, thinking of words that were never said.

A valley of giants looking over a ridge, a glimpse through time across a Crooked Bridge…

The Diary of Life

The stories of life are written in the sky, try to read them all before you die.

The air that breathes whispers a song, & the setting sun a portrait for days that seem long.

A taste of winter, a glimpse of spring, this is the beauty that Mother Nature brings.

A moment in time where life stands still, like a beautiful painting that somehow seems real.

Journeys that end & begin again, leave footsteps from the past that have no regrets.

The diary of life continues to write, beneath the moon & stars of light.

In the morning it breathes with the sun, & closes its eyes when the day is done.

Unbridled Dreams

A passionate dream of breaking free,
alone in my silent communication of things.

A vision of Beauty that steals my thoughts,
tangled in a web but not in knots.

A silent moment as dreams appear,
brings a quiet still attraction to my soul lying near.

Anonymously a whisper from somewhere in the dream,
unleashes a melody of an ocean stream.

Gaining a purpose without proposal,
a magical moment that comes to life.

Living a dream,
somewhere in my life…

Breaking Stones

What if candles in the wind were never meant to go out?
What if when you close your eyes the dreams that come take you
    away & never bring you back,
What if that already happened?
What if all the dreams made sense & what you dream is for all the
    right reasons?
What if dreaming is a way of sacrificing yourself in order to fulfill
    what is forgotten?
What if that which is remembered stays with the dream & is forgot-
    ten when you wake?
Does the dream repeat itself?
What if you dream out loud & lay in the fray of a broken day & what
    if you just breathe?

Save me from this madness!

Save me from the Breaking Stones that only exist in my own mind,
Searching for dreams that only exist when I close my eyes & when I
    dream out loud.

Escaping Fate

Is it possible to stop time?
If it's possible to stop time, then is it also possible to go back in time?
And if we can go back in time perhaps it's possible to change fate.

The mind and body have a specific purpose,
Just like the hands of a clock,
One cannot function without the other.
If there are no hands on the clock,
There is no way to keep track of time,
If there is no way to keep track of time,
Time does not exist.

If time does not exist,
Then fate does not exist.
If any of this is possible,
Then is it also possible there is a gateway to escaping fate…

Following Dreams

Dreams like blue shadows on the edge of night warm the soul like a
    Heavenly light.
A reservation for two where dreams come true, clouds undone where
    a light shines through.
Candles in the wind that never go out, dreams that whisper never
    shout.
Dreams that makes sense for all the right reasons, come to life like
    celebrating seasons.
Dreams that escape from days that are gone, reach the sky before the
    dawn.
Dreams that get lost in the right direction, dreams that wonder are
    life's perfection.
The tranquil moods of dreams release, silent footsteps open gates of
    peace.
Chasing dreams like an ongoing endeavor, following dreams into
    forever...

God & Time

If God is non-compliant to time, how then does time exist, and if time does not exist then how are we to be held accountable to time?

Time lives in the human realm but is non-existent in the spiritual.

Does that mean we have an endless supply of time?
Or is time just an illusion of non-compliance according to God?

Pretending time does not exist does not stop time, self-centered time is selfish and lives quietly by itself.

Pieces of time are valuable and running beyond time does not change the face of time, time does not require acceptance,

However, one must accept time in order to blend in with it.

Humbling yourself to God & time will slow the process of time,
But the only thing that can alter the course of time is Love.

God is Love & only God can stop time…

Passing Through Stopping at Life

I found myself on a long lonely road reinventing certain things in
    my life, things that only occur when all I have is time to think.

When I return to the place, I belong the occurrence of those things
    disappears and the invention gets scrapped, but only for a short
    time, only until the road returns.

The invention of those things slowly begins to rebuild itself, and I
    now find that time is short, but the long lonely road continues
    to grow.

I relax on my journey and try to take one day at a time, as difficult as
    it may seem I realize that what I am doing is,

Passing Through Stopping at Life…

The Brotherhood of Man

The sacred earth below his feet is a blanket of spiritual power that holds the secrets of Man & his connection with Mother Earth.

The word of the Holy Spirit has been read to many, but the Brotherhood of Man feels the Great Spirit from Mother Earth.

The words live in his soul and come to life, as the Four Winds, Sun, Earth, Water & Wind speak to him.

The Great Spirit gives him strength for his Warrior Soul,

As he stands in the Circle of Life, he prays to the East for warmth & the power of knowledge.

As he turns to the South, he prays for power to grow & peace in the world.

As he faces the West, he prays for purity & strength.

As he prays to the North, he gives thanks to the Great White Cleansing Wind & prays for the wisdom of experience.

As the Great Wolf & the Mighty Buffalo stand with him in the Circle of Life,

They become One in the Brotherhood of Man.

The Hourglass of Time

When the angels come, do they take you by the hand and lead you
to the Gates of Heaven?

To the Promised Land?
To spend eternity with God.

Are your sins forgiven with His Unconditional Love?
Do the Angels sing the songs that we hear from Heaven above?

Your hourglass of time has dropped its last grain, no more tears, no
more pain.

Our loss is Heaven's gain.

Though we will miss you in our hourglass of time, you will always
live in our hearts and in our minds.

Time spent with you seemed Heaven sent,
God's gift to us, you were only lent.

You will always live in our hearts & our dreams,
You were here for a short time, or so it seems…

The Oak Tree

It was early November under that old oak tree,
The Vision of God came to me.

We talked about life & the creation of new birth,
We talked about the creatures that walk the earth.

We talked about His Son that gave His Blood,
We talked about Noah & the Mighty flood.

We talked about things & places I've been,
We talked about Love, I told Him of my sin.

He told me about Heaven & how it would be,
He told me about the place He prepared for me.

He told me about the people in Heaven, family & friends,
He told me about how time never ends.

He told me these things, a vision I could see,
He told me these things under that

Old Oak Tree...

The Old Man

I came across a man in great despair,
Ripped jeans he had no hair,

His shirt was torn, his shoes a disgrace,
The road map of life was on his face,

I stood in wonder as he sat there,
It suddenly occurred to me, life isn't fair.

I threw some change in his can, thoughts raced through my mind,
"Why has God forgotten this man?"

With a gleam in his eyes and a smile on his face he said to me;
"God thanks you for your Grace."

With joy in my heart I dared to stare,
That could be me sitting there.

As I walked on once more to stare,
The Old Man was no longer there,

On Angel Wings his Soul took flight;
That was an Angel that sat there that night…

The Tree of Life

~The empty spaces in my mind are quickly filled with the image of an inescapable place that comes to me at night.

~As I listen to the sounds of silence, I hear the echoing cries of a life from long ago.

~Many have walked by the Tree of Life, but few have ever embraced its beauty & spiritual power.

~As I walk along the forest floor, the rustling sound of the leaves embracing my footsteps is like a symphony in harmony with God & nature.

~The image revealed to me is like a mirror of my past, leading me to the future, realizing that the Tree of Life is actually a place that lives in my mind.

~Soaring deeper into this image, I find myself near a journey's end, surrounded by beauty, & yet my mind will take me no further.

~As the air is silent & my soul is at peace, I feel as if I am standing at the entrance to a Holy Kingdom.

~As my body is frozen in time, I find myself, not at journey's end, but yet at the beginning, not only in my mind, but buried deep in my soul,

~I have found the Tree of Life…

Vision Quest

When I close my eyes the curiosity of my mind takes over all living thoughts of an inescapable dream that is impossible to catch.

Being chased by my past keeps the dream alive to keep running toward the entrance of another dream that has not been invented yet.

My mind can recognize this place, but my hand cannot touch what is not there. So, I dreamscape to a place that does not exist.

Frozen in this dream I realize there is no escape.

Surrounded by Angels in a forest of dreams I find myself heading to the entrance of Heaven.

The past is no longer chasing me, so I walk, but there are no footsteps left behind.

When I open my eyes, the dream disappears.

My Mind speaks to my Soul and the image revealed to me is a

Vision Quest.

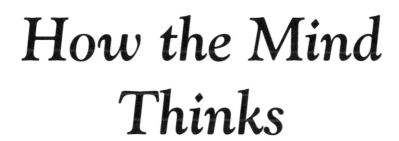

How the Mind Thinks

Yvonne Hewitt

Who would've known so long ago?
Your two lives would turn into many
Fifty plus years together you had
Adding four daughters along the way to your family

Raised them to be independent and strong
Not to be fake to prove they belong
Then they gave you 17 grandchildren
Then great and great greats, too many to mention

Your strengths, love and wise teachings
Passed down from generation to generation

Who would've known so long ago?
Your two lives would turn into many
I know I'm glad the list is long
Thanks to you this family is forever strong

Breaking at the seams
Holding onto all my dreams
Fighting to breath
And dying to scream

Trying to remember
Praying for an ember
Looking towards Orion
And feeling like an ion

Walking to the future
Feeling no more pressure
Finding a new adventure
And a love that lasts…

Forever

I see you staring at me,
But never truly see.
Why do I love you?
When you're so far out of reach.
Feelings we could have shared,
You flung them without a care.
I don't know whether I should stay
And waste yet another day
I know that all this pain
Will soon drive me insane
You don't feel me loving you
And you can't let me through
You don't see me cry inside
And in you I can't confide
You are still so blind
To things meant to be kind
You know nothing of my fears
And are unaware of all my tears
Every time I look at your face
For me there's never any space
Maybe someday you'll see me differently
So, until then, I'll be waiting silently

So many questions, no answers to give
Will the blahness in life ever end
We try to keep positive for the loves in our lives
Living day to day, doing everything right

Babies getting diagnosed with cancer
Brain surgeons ending up with Alzheimer's
The good always dying way before they should
While the bad keep walking freely abroad

So dark are these thoughts
I know that's what you think
But how true this is
The words that I speak

If this is how life is supposed to be
Why are we here
Why doesn't this world end?
So many questions, no answers to give

My heart is hurting
Full of loved ones lost
The crap that follows
Why are people so harsh?

I need to find peace
Within this world
…within myself
Why is this world so dark?

I cry at night
Smile throughout the day
If everyone only knew
The emptiness I feel inside

Why can't they see
The hurt that I feel
The pain that keeps stabbing
The sorrow the guilt

The sadness always takes over
These tears I try to hold back
Hopefully soon this is over
And happiness I will never lack

Some days are good
Some days are bad
I miss you my friend
I want you back

I guess he needed you
Though I needed you more
Why couldn't he let you stay
Until "I" was ready to let you soar

Our inside jokes
And little snickers
Read each other's minds
With a look, an eyebrow flicker

The times we shared
The drinks and dances
Our secrets still in my head

I want you back
I miss you my friend

As big as the world
Your heart size is
Seen in your eyes, smiles
And kindness to friends

Some will take advantage
Try to break you down
You are better than that
Don't you ever frown

Keep your smiles big
And your heart huge
Good things will always come
And the negative ones will lose

Years will go by
And soon you will see
Your kindest of heart
Is what this world needs

You consider yourself a man
You call yourself a dad
You put a ring on her finger
So, a family you have
Your nose in the game
No money being made
No smiles you have given
Just harsh words and hushes
Your "loved" one's hearts crushing

You are selfish and worthless
Leaving your better half all the burden
When YOU should be providing
Being a good dad and husband

Your titles are due to gender
Not anything other
Maybe you should go back in your mother
And try starting life all over

The clouds float in
The sun is gone
Snowflakes fall
Why is winter so long

Depression sets in
Sun where are you my friend
I need your light
Winter please end

Spring is so needed
Let cleanups begin
The smell of fresh air
Bad thoughts out of my head

Daffodils blooming
Birds singing instead
The warmth of summer sun
Oh, shit its Fall again

The clouds float in
The sun is gone
Snowflakes fall
Why is winter so long

I hear your laughter
It makes my heart happy
I hear you cry
It makes my heart sad

I'll make it go away
I'll promise you that
No more sad days
I can't handle that

So, joy in your life
Is the only thing allowed?
You'll be strong and succeed
I'll be forever proud

Now when you cry
Its tears of joy that I see
I promise you this
And forever it will be

Poetry Time

Lorrie West

He slowly wipes her
tears as he can hear
her cry wonders of love
starting to show as he
sits listening to the words of tears

Beauty of life

The beauty of life
as the wind blows
through time as words whisper
another thought
as the day plays so long
as the tree blows its leaves
with time the beauty of life

White house

Pillars of gold days sold
red white and blue and so true
a queen with a dance and dollars to pay
the way
soldiers standing tall for a country
beauty of stars to light the night and day
in the window played the party
as everyone could see the
drunk of luck

Some days

When I fall in love
like to little birds
singing away in the day
will you love me too?
someday I'll love
with words to tell and
moments to cry about
I'll kiss you like a little
bird swing away in the day

Angel

As the flag shines its angel
red white and blue
stars so bright in the light
love moves the world
in time we see a country
standing tall with all
with a golden crown and a frown
to face falling angels

The first Lady of Elizabeth

A moment in the day
thought with time
life in beauties like
flowers to grow
holding on tie with
love to be
far in time a moment
to share as the day soon
comes to an end

The Flower

The flower in time
blooming to say the beauty
of god to shine
as words are many and time is short
listen to the rain fall in life
as the flower blooms another note
far away in the distance of the day
shining a flower today

America

God stands for her country
loving the beauty
red white and blue
stars shining bright
for all to see
a ship to sail on the land
of time empires build
for a queen to be
America

The Rose

The Princess rose
beauty of love
petals of time fall down from
her heart as stem of green cover
the ground and wind chime in the
music she sung with love she
holds them close to her nose as the
smell of perfume came with time
the rose

Nature

The nature that sings
through the windows of eyes
watching as birds fly to
the winter days as the sun
speaks a moment of joy it's all
dead now as the cold has left
us all lonely now

Whispering

Whispering words of love
as I love you so in the
beauty of my heart I hold
you close with though of
you and me I whisper many
words of love

Her Beauty

She was silent as a rose
beauty of petals in the
leaves of green shine in her windows
of love
pink glory filled the way
as moments sit away
as he was stairs in time
with love to climb
her beauty was frame like
a picture

Flowers

Flowers of beauty
sit in silence with days to know
green leaves blowing in the wind
with thoughts to bring about
walks to take on a fresh moment
perfume beauty spread around the path
as life has brightened our way

Strong

He walked so strong
in the shadows of his eyes
lurk the beast of tomorrow dreams

Sea

The great sea of god's
washing away tomorrow's dream's
like a ship to sail the beauty
as the skies are so blue for you and me
sand dollars on the shore
step of god coming and going
wishing you were here

A Moment

Only in the moment
do we share our love?
like a rose petal to the sea
with waves crashing in on us all

will tomorrow bring another day
of sad thoughts and mad words
of the world we live like
god above

Prayer

Only with god do we cry in prayer
as god knows today the
troubles we bear
Only with god I pray to the world
only with god in the heart of lamb and
wool of a sheep standing on the mountain
with time to climb

God Love

Guide me to the
place as god loves
his only son
say a prayer for the lord above
listen to the day as the
words flow for the tomorrow beauty
cover in rain and snow
the cold comes and goes
deep in my heart I love you so
like the flower to shine
the ways of me and you

To Grow

To grow like mom
in a vase of life
with water and sunlight
to grow like mom
planted like a seed with
weeds to pull as the garden
freshen are way today

Grace

I try to write to grace again
I saw her tears as I slowly wiped mine away
I said to her in a poet of words
how I would miss her in light of it all
I know there's no other as I slowly wipe another tear
I turn to know her as I know she is turning gray
I said to her as I pray away
to keep this thought of my son
In the distance time
God Bless

Voices in
the Dark

Special thanks to Leslie Wingard.

TOM DECARME

Try as you might, you can't force it.
Someone must have said it at one time, and yet.
Time after time someone tries to do just that.
How can we as humans afford to wait?
You cannot hold time, but we constantly try to save it.
As if it was ever ours to save. Only God can create time and yet we
    try to make it.
In time someone can go around and around and still go nowhere.
People do it every time, all the time. So, I sit here and waste time in
    a pale
Attempt to convince myself I do indeed have. For what?
So, we want to force ourselves on time.
Try as we might and before you know it your out of time.
But we had our time.

I look at the world with an alien eye.
I see it different, hostite somehow.
Could I really be part of it?
Eb and Flow the clock ticks and one seems to move forward a notch.
To where?
It's unknown but often thought about.
Does it really matter?
I Love You…

The night wind screams the cry of forgotten souls long past, as the
full moon watches on and laughs with a skeleton grin.
I'm sure the graves are restless tonight.
Do you hear the scratching on the box?
Don't smile it could be the scratching in your own head you hear…
LET ME OUT!
The dead howl past a darkened window breathing their ghostly foul
fog.
Obscuring the light of life, love…forever…
Can you feel it as a spider crawls across your face?
Leaving no light,
No life.
Not a trace…

Then there is my boy…
Boy do I feel incomplete. Not a provider, or taker or giver of meat.
He waits all snaggle toothed and grim.
His world, his water, his way and he waits.
My prehistoric friend. Hang tight. Hang tuff till the very end.
Guess the rest.
You past the test my simulator, my alligator.
Raymond the Cayman a.k.a. the breather from Manayunk, Philly PA
I love him and will never forget him.
That is my way…

Killed or wounded, 5000 strong possible more. Heavy waves, blood
     cloud explosion. Churning on itself, lead grey easy red.
Jaw naws so I saw, his eyes dead, ripped back and forth. Ragdoll
     romance he will no longer dance.
Ears ring loud sounds of the macobe. Distraught, don't we love it.
He's dead, he's dead so they said.
But the Finn did not care.
Cutting the water, cutting the flesh, cutting whatever it wants.
Who could move? Not I.

Smack acid blur. Blue breus rises, shades of purple sky draws your
     attention but still you don't listen.
Primal fear dark and distant scratching on the inside of your Skull
     like Nails on a chalkboard.
Still your ignored. You can kill and still end up a victim. Twisted and
     crushed. Pulverized into
Exactly what they wanted you to be. Still you don't see.
Smack acid clear.
Tummers settle in and make themselves at home. Time is on their
     side. Suck your own piece of paranoia.
They'll destroy ya…

You can hide but you can't run and it's exactly the way they want you
     to be and you are.
No longer able to breath. I know what I need.
Smack acid miracle.
The Fight will go on, Methodical, devastating, Miniecle old habits
     hard to brake.
Lots to be shown we die alone…

SMASH! And eventually everything did.
We all looked like we told you so.
But it's forever predictable, the bullet hits the tooth.
Shattered blood splatter.
Look at the pattern.
I say ok, that's a joke and it all stops.
A new genus of a silent taker.
A killer walks among us.
A Genghis Khan of sorts.
Smell it in the air? …I don't care…

Love, Trust.
Cold, Lust.
Pump, Thrust.
Slip in, not Sin
We win.
Baby!

Dactile, reptile, no style.
We sit we stare, we smile. I'll kiss you latter.
We sip sunsets while the sky's on Fire.
Couldn't get much higher I suppose.
Fingers locked in a kaleidoscope weave, fast and hard never let go.
Primeval shots in the dark, disembark, descend.
It all depends on the timing.
We must watch our step my friend.
Fading fast, everlast the futures now forget the past.
10 years. Salt solution hart pollution.
Fait screams for some retribution. Yeah dude.

Suck that bottle. Before you know it, it has started sucking you. This
time you pray it doesn't swallow. Still you follow.

Body racked your deck has been stacked. You limp like a beginner, a
spoiled sinner destined for disaster.

Follow your own trail of blood. You see Your own dead spot, now
stand in it.

Compleat…

That bottles my friend.

My end, my final Justice.

My fair-weather friend. See You on the other side soon! You hope
not…

But, you will. Oh, you will.

What can I say, I fucked my cock raw the other day?

Illusions of Grandeur I will not pander to you.

So, take your sarcasm and move along.

How important are we anyway?

To have time wasted on us as if we deserve it.

What should I think? It's Pink.

Threw a hole too your Soul. Hallucinations are real.

Randum and violent feelings, watch your dealings.

I'd be more spot on, but I don't want to be boring or too revealing.

How should I be? Swollen lips tell the tail now I'm pail.

My heart does flippity-flops, incredible chops. Mental shops.

Self help yourself.

Simple words pop like turds and roll down a shoot on to my paper
    smell my vaper.
What kind of sick shit is that?
Puffy stools firing from the assholes of our minds.
Torpedoes to a target, like a sperm to an egg they will find the way.
Do you have something to say?
How about more on the floor PLOP! There it is, roll around in it it's
    all you man.
My mind is there when it wants to be. Come look for me if you dare!
Better yet I'll come looking for you.
I want to climb around in your head.
I'm dead.

Lack of discipline is killing me, thrilling me. Somehow for filling me.
I guess I was never really meant to last long, is there anyone that is!
Hear your brain FIZZ.
Lack of insight why do we fight? Are We getting through to each
    other?
Do you, are you getting me? Or I you? What else should we do?
Feelings that are real I can't feel at least I wish.
Sardonic components cop with donuts, Watch it! They will grab a
    hold.
Bodies poled, impaled on their own point they try to make.
My mistake, my bad so sad I will cry all night over that one.
It's all in fun.
Father and son reach the sun. Don't let your wings burn off.
Lack of sill eventually spills Our lives unwheeling, life with no ceiling
    how revealing.
Go suck yourself for a feeling…

Alien hand syndrome!
Nightmare who cares!
Alien hand is gonna set you straight, horror and hate.
Rotted Ccrpse stairs in silence. Dead men tell no tales bill inhales.
Electro sonic. Corpusculum. Brain is bionic. Midnight tonic.
Hear no evil, see no evil have no fun. know no better.
Folklore, murder victim makes us scaredterror aired brain surgery
dared now alien hand. Understand?…

I love my cat that is what commonly is known as that.
He's like a little man from another planet, furry body eyes slanted.
We hang out a lot me and him.
Talking, walking. Not doing much of anything really.
We fight we play I tickle away not much else to say.
He's my boy, my main man and I am his.
Only to be second to a shiny metal can. But I'm still the man, you
      dig…
I've had many friends like him. Both guys and girls. They come and
      they go
My feline friends do.
But I remember them all when I let out with a call. DINK, DINK,
      DINK!!! Come on! Get in here
And eat ya little poopers!

Do you remember when my dark-haired friend so many years have
 passed.
Memory's awash with time.
Do you remember why those big dark eyes would laugh and dance
 across skies.
When love seemed possible and life an eternity.
We'd roll around in wet grass and boast of our love.
Do you remember how you'd laugh so loud like a Parrot, drinking
 rum?
Sailing fare from me now, let go of my hand. Time to leave.
And now I let your memory go.
But never forever, nor to fast.
Always slow.

High as kite, city lights cat fights.
Cries carry down an alley does anyone hear it?
Colors collide, explode as one when you smear it.
Decadence knows no bounds, graveyard grounds.
Can you hear it.
Heave rocks at your own world. My world's done.
Ramble on ramble on. Singing that song. I already did.
I'm done.
I'm out.

I have an idol that's like a spider in my brain.
It's driving me insane.
That I just have to tell you about it.
But I must catch it first.
Got a cup?

Is this who you are? Are you sure? Do you really know without a doubt?
Without hesitation. For real…Or is it who you tell yourself you are.
How long can we ask that question?
A bastard in the realm of Idols.
A contradiction in terms.
A mellow drama played out every day. How passed and yet unfath-
　　omable and forgotten.
What's your real deal?
I don't think we know do we. Ask yourself.
Ask yourself a real question for once and tell the truth.
If there is such a thing.

You're so politically correct. So, erect with Your opinions and views.
Full cycle, you imitate the ones you hate don't you. look at yourself
　　for second.
Are you for real? Really. Don't get all touchy feely! I mean really…
The more you teach the more you preach.
Gone baby, gone your all wrong.
Losing touch with the very people You try to reach.
How many bridges do we have to cross to see the big boss?
Written on a London wall, says it all.

Little Girl Lost

Little girl lost is not for me.
I am exactly where I want to be.
Time's a distraction simplified to the T.
I know exactly when I need to be.
A distressed damsel will never be me.
I know exactly what I'm supposed to be.
No little girl lost.
No little girl lost!
I know exactly what my attitude cost.
Reaching the glory is worth it to me.
I am exactly where I want to be.

Norma Von Reichenbach-Nichols — March 11. 2009.

Life

Reggie Harris

Time Flies Fast

As the sunsets, so does the days pass, hour after hour, time flies fast.
Like sand in an hour glass, little by little, time flies fast.
Like a fast car, foot on the gas, you can't stop it, time flies fast.
As we enter the future, exit the past, in a blink of an eye, time flies
    fast.
If you're on a plane, that's bout to crash, (literally), time flies fast.
Like a cloudy day, with an overcast, as the clouds rolls, time flies fast.
With nothing to stop it or make it last, there's one thing we know,
    time really flies fast.

Drug Addiction

Addiction is not a disease it's a choice, everybody has an option, just
     listen to that little voice.
You know the one that speaks to you inside your head, warning you
     of the forth-coming troubles that lies ahead.
But still you choose otherwise instead, and give in, just to please what
     you love and crave.
Drugs off the streets, imagine how many lives we'll save, but that's
     only in a perfect world, so prepare more coffins for the grave.
Years of addition got you set in your ways, unwilling to change, just
     means you'll soon be dead.
Lord help, cause most of them are out their heads, can you tell by
     their actions and how they behave.
Most love drugs more than they love themselves, it's a shame that
     they love their addiction to death.
But I guess that's the problem, free will have no restrictions, most peo-
     ple don't realize that their addiction is their own self-infliction.

Strong Woman

You're forever sacrificing, always putting yourself on hold, you always put the family first, your job never gets old.

You're a solid foundation, the household cornerstone, you're the strength of the family, the family backbone.

There's so much you deal with, struggling and juggling, between work, kids, and school, not to mention if you're married, dealing with a complaining husband and his rules.

But somehow, some way, you continue to chug along, dealing with the troubles of life, it's amazing how you remain strong.

As time repeats itself, everyday it's the same task, for the love and happiness of your family, you'll sacrifice everything and always give your last.

Men are clueless, most don't comprehend, what it means to be a woman and all the drama that it brings.

Hard times and heartache, abandonment, living you're alone, sometimes you're a single mother and a father, if there's no man in the home.

It's an ongoing story for any woman with this scare, but just in case you're wondering, be proud, because a beautiful strong woman is what you are.

As A Man

As a man, I rely on no man to keep me standing upright, I plan to stand on my own two feet and use no one as my crutch through life.

As a man, I'll never portray the role of someone else, whether you accept me or not, I'll forever be true to myself.

As a man, I'll support what I believe in and show respect the one's I love, I'll die for them if necessary, but only if it requires blood.

As a man, I'm dedicated to my family, so I'm obligated to be loyal, I try teaching them all the right things and give them all the best things I can offer.

As a man, it's either I hate it or love it, I'll love it or leave it, it's either I want it or I don't, because there's no in between it.

As a man, I vow death before dishonor and loyalty before betrayal, I know trust means everything, but honesty and love will never fail.

As a man, these are the things I shall live and die by, but of course as a man I do realize, that not everyone lives by these standards like, I.

Believe in You

Many will criticize you, some will be doubtful, but ignore the nay-sayer's and don't let nothing stop you.

For there's always skepticism and hate in the pursuit of happiness, so be clever, be smart, be above the average list.

Be at your best when presenting your skills, though they may try to kill your spirit, you can't allow them to kill your will.

Use your drive and motivation as your fuel going forward in life, utilize all your resources and always stay focus on the prize in sight.

Know where you're headed, set your goals in line, keep your priorities straight and make good use of your time.

Hurdle the obstacles, that's ahead in front, never give up or in, until you've retrieved what you want.

Move at a steady pace, but proceed with caution, know that success comes from hard work, dedication and tireless exhaustion.

Know that it doesn't matter what people may say or put you through, just remember you can achieve anything, long as you believe in you.

Beautiful

If beauty lie's in the eyes of the beholder, then beauty is all I see,
    unexplainable, un-comparable, is how you appear to me.
Your looks, your smile, the way it light's up your eyes, your beauty is
    hard to put in words and even harder for me to describe.
It's no secret, (beautiful) you attract men in a strong way, so innocent
    and unaware of the beauty that you display.
I feel I can honestly say, given the opportunity, any man should be
    willing to marry you today.
And there's nothing to dispute, a beautiful woman like you deserves
    the world, and that's the God holy truth.

Crucified

Stone him, torcher him, it won't change a thing, hate him, kill him, set him to flames.

This is what you do when you slander his name, regardless how you crucify him, it's all the same.

Call me crazy, but I think it's insane, for folks to enjoy other folk's sufferings, when they have nothing to gain.

What a shame, how selfish and ridiculous this world has become, all the intentional hurt, for reasons that they can't explain.

All the jealousy and envy start's in the heart and stems into the brain, just another flaw, to show the imperfection of a man.

No one knows what exist in the mind of a man, what he's feeling, what he's thinking, whether he's living in pain.

So, before you crucify him, try to understand, you can't judge him for what he was, but only for what he's became.

My Character

My character defines me, it's who I am, it's everything I stand for, day
    to day as a man.
It's my description, my lifestyle and all, it's what separates me from
    others and allows me to evolve.
Into the person that I am, into the man that you see, my character
    keeps me going, it keeps me being me.
From the way I behave, to the mood I display, this who I am, it's not
    an image I portray.
Regardless of what I do, regardless of what I say, my character a never
    change, this is me every day.
So, judge me how you may, but it's clear and easy to see, my character
    is who I am, it's the perfect replica of me.

Roses

A rose for a rose, what a flower that I chose, there are a bunch of different flowers, but none like a rose.

From its stem, to its thrones, all the way up to its petals, the beauty of a rose is sure to bring us together.

A rose, each unique in it's on way, a bouquet of roses, is sure to brighten someone's day.

From the scent, to the softness of its touch, when I think of the beauty a rose, I have no choice but think of us.

It's a special flower, for that special someone, who's in your every thought, I don't need the keys to anything, only if these roses can earn me the keys to your heart.

Some Kind of Woman

After all he put you through, you still stood firm, unwilling to leave
    his side, unwilling to let it all burn.
With so many opportunities, you could've thrown it all away, plus
    everything that he did, gave you every reason not to stay.
All the late-night auguring, that led to the morning fights, problem
    after problem with him, became the story of your life.
I can only imagine how stressful it was, it's obvious to see, that you
    were really fighting for love.
So, my hats off to you, I admire your love for him, to deal with that
    kind of chaos, you are some kind of a woman.

African Skin

Here I am, nothing more, nothing less, whether you hate me or love me, regardless I'm still blessed.

Blessed for who I am and blessed for what I represent, a proud black man, loving this remarkable color of my skin.

Forget how I appear to the world and to the eyes of some men, long as I love myself and I know what lives within.

And that's love, honor, and dignity; accompanied by pride, respect, and of course intelligence, it's all part of black history.

Thinking of our past, sometimes can bring misery, but we must to learn to forgive and forget, try to throw it out of your memories.

So regardless what transpires today or happened back then, I'm still proud to be an American, representing and loving this African Skin.

Family

Family, it's the one thing that keeps us tired together, generations of
　　bloodlines that you can trace back forever.

Whether you nearby or far away, separated or close, everybody should
　　know the importance of family and what matters the most.

And that's loving and bonding together, that can't ever be erased,
　　an inseparable connection, knowing that family can never be
　　replaced.

Your brothers, your sisters, your mom and dad, your kids and pretty
　　much everybody that's related to you, is all you have.

For them, I'm sure you would give up all you have, just to see them
　　happy and healthy, plus able to smile and laugh.

So, despite the negativity and all the bull they hand me, I'll do my
　　best not to let anything come between me and my family.

Greater Plans

Through all my ups and downs, even when life give me every reason to frown, somehow, I still believe that God has greater plans.

Through all my trials and tribulations, regardless of how bad the situation that I might be facing, somehow, I still believe that God has greater plans.

Through all my troublesome days of feeling ill, as I'm fighting stay alive and continue to live, somehow, I still believe that God has greater plans.

Through the constant battles and my uphill climbs, in situations where help is hard to find, somehow, I still believe that God has greater plans.

When I'm alone and no one's there, and my life's in total despair, somehow, I still believe that God has greater plans.

When I'm dead broke, without any help or support, somehow, I still believe that God has greater plans.

So, if you're going something and you feel like all hope is lost, just try to remember that somehow, God has greater plans.

Eternal Life

Joy to the world, let it be peace on earth, may the good lord bless,
    every man created from dirt.
Let the songs we sing, bring joy to our hearts, may it uplift our spirits
    and shed light in the dark.
For we all are blessed, by the loving grace of God, in which we all are
    saved, through Jesus Christ our lord.
Sacrifices were made, so that our sins would be forgiven, by our lord
    and savior, who from the grave was risen.
Trust in the almighty and believe every word he said, though we shall
    die, but through him we shall never be dead.
Blessed be the lord, who paid the ultimate price, he saved us from
    ourselves and blessed us with gift of eternal life.

Empty

When you've been driven to the point of no return, living and dying
    seems to be your least concern.

It's that moment right there, your world stalls to turn, darkness sets
    in and your soul starts to burn.

Sad to say, but it all starts within, a few problems in life, can turn
    fools into a bunch of heartless men.

Cold-heartedness and bitterness can damage the soul, leave you with
    a miserable feeling, causing you to lose control.

With nothing to live for or no reason to go on, is a bad combination
    of thoughts, planted in the mind of a man, who heart is torn.

So, I won't allow those feelings to tempt me, because I'm well-aware
    of all the ingredients, that drive people to feeling empty.

Life

Life, what can better, what more can you expect, other than a great feeling of being blessed.

Blessed to live, blessed to love, blessed with life, and even better, blessed with the love of Christ.

Life, it's God's greatest gift to man, created in his own image by the work of his hands.

So regardless of who you are or whence you came, you have the gift of life, so just enjoy it while you can.

Everyday won't be great and there'll be some things you don't understand, but living is worth every moment, even when you're going through pain.

God makes no mistakes, so let that be clear, if you living to see today, there's a special reason that you're here.

So, do what's necessary and let your light shine bright, be thankful for every moment, because you've been blessed with the great gift of life.

Cancer

Listen, we can research it, discuss it, or debate it, but the fact remains, cancer is still one of the top killers and we hate it.

May God curse where it from or how it originated, it's a human destroyer, and finding a cure is way outdated.

We need it now, that's an understatement, don't believe me, just ask any cancer patient.

This disease spreads fast with no hesitation, progressing aggressively, destroying everyone in its path, and it's not waiting.

I commend the doctors for their efforts, because they're appreciated, but every time someone dies, it proves that their time was wasted.

This is ridiculous, it's really-outrageous, to still not have a cure, to cure these patients.

Thank God, that it's not contagious, but neither is it prejudice, and it doesn't care a thing about racism.

As the search continues, this sickness continues to move on, it's a death sentence and it's approaching every home.

So, when it comes to finding a cure, there's nothing more I'd rather, it's time for science and medicine to find an answer, for this plague called cancer.

Through My Eyes

Through my eyes, I see the destruction of mankind, for the love of money, some folks a sell their souls for a dime.

Through my eyes, I can see the racial hate, that still exist in the world, as of today.

Through my eyes, I've witnessed hardship and hard times, the everyday struggles, the uphill climbs.

Through my eyes, I can see the horror, that takes place in the world, leaving families living in sorrow.

Through my eyes, I see the sufferings of others, so many problems and troubles, soon as they overcome one thing, they encounter another.

Through my eyes, I've seen how a war can destroy a life, so many dead and wounded soldiers, because power and freedom come at a horrible price.

Through my eyes, I've witnessed the terror, I've seen so many terrible things, but with so much unfortunate pleasure.

From the Ground

From the ground I can see it all, I see nations rising, as others fall.

I see the economic crisis within the nations, disputes and disagreements, it's a complicated situation.

What use to be peaceful living, has become a struggle to survive, it's every man for himself, even the innocent die.

It's total chaos and death show's no pity, there's killings everywhere and it's happening in every small town and in every big city.

Everyday it's the same thing, time changes with the seasons, but people remain the same, killing for whatever reason.

They say seeing is believing, then this all I see, a world in need of some serious healing.

And me, well let's just say, I've been up, and I've been down, although I see things much clearer from the top, I observe things much better here from the ground.

Only Because

You're my everything, my little piece of heaven, you're my angel, sent
   to make my life pleasant.
Long as you live, I shall never love again, there isn't another human I
   desire, from now until the end.
As I stare into your eyes, I hope it's written on my face, that my love,
   my commitment, will never stray away.
Words cannot describe, what I'm trying to say, it's hard to put in
   words, what I feel for you every day.
Only for your love, I'll make this sacrifice, to change who I am and
   redirect my life.
You complete me, so therefore I'll always cherish you, I don't do this
   just because, but only because I love you.

Life as I See It

It's said that life is what you make of it, how far you go, depends on
how well you plan for it.

Well if that's the case, the question is why haven't we all found suc-
cess, most people live a typical mediocre life at best.

We primary blue-collar workers, working a regular nine to five, living
day to day, check to check, constantly struggling to survive.

Now I know life is about choices, just as well as the chances we take,
but most of us don't have many options, so that interferes and
alters some of the decisions we make.

Life to me, is very unbalanced, how can we ever be stable when we're
overloaded with a lot more than we can handle.

Stress, problems, and poverty are the main things that troubles and
bothers us, and it's even worse when it continues to follow us.

And I understand that not everyone can be rich, but everyone hates
to be poor, so tell me what's the difference between a house with
no ceiling and a house with no floors.

Nothing actually, they're both incomplete, so whether you rich or
poor, one can't exist without the other, and that's life and how
it appears to me.

Why Settle

Why settle, when you know what you deserve, even as you age, you're
like fine wine that's preserved.
Why settle, for anything other than number one, you should have
first options and be second to none.
Why settle, when you shouldn't settle for less, it's not your fault, if he
doesn't recognize what's best.
Why settle, when you can have what you want, trust that there's
someone who sees' your value even if you don't.
Why settle, when you simply don't have to, I'm pretty sure there's
someone else that's wishing they had you.
Why settle, when it's easy to see, the fool that had you is just as blind
as can be.
But why settle, isn't really the question, you don't have to settle is
really my message.

My Heart

My heart, my world, my everything, what I feel for you, makes me
wanna sing.

It's no secret, I can't conceal what I feel within, cause what I feel
inside, I can't comprehend.

All I know, it's something I never felt before, and it's a feeling, I don't
wanna ever let go.

Whether I'm feeling high or low, you lift me up, allows me to func-
tion and go.

And I don't care if the world is ready to know, cause what I feel, I'm
ready to show.

For you, I'll let it all go, I've had a taste of your love and now I'm
ready for more.

So, I can't fake it, I can't lie, and I won't pretend, I want you forever
even if it means living in sin.

Sunrise

As I lie awake, daylight peeks through my blinds, it's morning and
the sun just begun to climb.

What a beautiful scenery, as the sun begins to rise, the beautiful sun
rays, reflected across the sky.

It's a sight to see, to witness with your eyes, it's a beautiful day, a
beautiful feeling to be alive.

Caught in the moment, you can get lost in time, this beautiful set-
ting, is the perfect way to ease your mind.

Mother nature can help, with the peace you seek to find, you can see
it for yourself, its displayed in the sky.

Like an artist with a vision, painting an image in your mind, a mas-
terpiece, only to be revealed in time.

This God's work, every morning, same time, this is him at his best,
putting his touches across the sky.

What Do You Care

What do you care, Mr. Over achiever, Mrs. Non-believer, who doesn't
   believe in nothing or no one else, but themselves.
What do you care, whether who lives or dies, when you and yours
   steady living it up, enjoying your lives.
What do you care, whether my family starves or not, you so quick to
   pass judgement, but it's not like you helping us out.
What do you care, Mr. Know It All, Mrs. Show It Off, Mr. and Mrs.
   I'm On Top of The World and we won't ever fall off.
What do you care, when our troubles are not yours, our problems are
   in plain sight, but it's things you choose to ignore.
What do you care, Mr. and Mrs. Politicians, who's only goal and
   mission, is to persuade people to vote, if you can convince them
   to listen.
What do you care, really, I don't think you care at all, because if you
   did, you wouldn't be standing there watching us fall.

With You

With you, I can do no wrong, not only am I protected, but I'm also sheltered from all angles of harm.

With you, I can weather any storm, I have no worries, no anxieties, I'm happy and calm.

With you, I'm like a flower in the spring time, I can blossom and prosper into something unique and divine.

With you, I'm always able to find peace, your word not only gives me strength, but it's my weaponry against the beast.

With you, I'm strong, I'm solid, nothing about me is hollow, wherever you go, I'm willing to follow.

With you, it's easy to identify the truth, I'm confident and capable of leading the youth.

With you, there's isn't anything I can't overcome, cause trying to live without you, let me is just plain dumb.

Without You

Without you, I'm just as lost as I can be, I have no since of direction,
   my whole life feels incomplete.

Without you, I'm blind as a bat, feeling my way through the dark,
   not knowing where I'm at.

Without you, is living without faith, it's like a nightmare, I can't
   escape, nor awake.

Without you, I'm like a sheep living amongst the wolves, that moved
   out of the pasture to go live the woods.

Without you, my heart is empty, my life is carefree, I'm hopeless and
   unable to see.

Without you, my chances of survival are slim and none, I'm like a
   soldier at war, with an empty gun.

Without you, there's so much that can go wrong, because trying to
   live without you, there's no way life can go on.

Last Request

As I stood beside him, I could almost see it in his face, that any moment, any time, any day could be the day.

I heard him cry out, as if he was shouting from far away, fighting with every breathe to get out all last words he wanted to say.

And in that moment, I knew he was slowly slipping away, unwilling to accept reality, I immediately started to pray.

Praying for a man, I came to know in such a short while, a man of strong spiritual faith and who encouraged me through my trials.

A man in my opinion, who gave God every reason to smile and be proud, though he were just a man, when it came to God, he was obedient as a child.

How and why, are the thoughts that continued to drift through my mind, in search of an answer I don't have and couldn't seem to find.

Why, I can't live with the fact that we all have a time, and just face reality, that we all will die.

In a state of disbelief, trying to gather my head, it just doesn't feel real, I can't believe that he's dead.

But nevertheless, I know he wouldn't want me to stress, so I'll just do my best, to keep the promises I made, and honor a dying man's last request.

Heart of A Man

In the heart of a man, lies many things, his joy, his pain, all his innermost secrets, his thoughts and feelings that he keeps in concealment.

In the heart of a man, you may find and discover, what brings him happiness, also what keeps him troubled and puzzled.

In the heart of a man, there's much to know, much to learn, like his most cherished possessions, and his most fearsome concerns.

In the heart of a man, you'll see what provokes his actions, what interests him, what brings him complete satisfaction.

In the heart of a man, you'll learn what makes him the man he is, where he gets his courage, what's his greatest fears.

In the heart of a man, what's to discover is so much, like who is nearest and dearest to him, who he really loves and trust.

In the heart of a man, you'll find what he believes in, all his goals and plans, all the reasons for which he stands.

In the heart of a man, you can learn a lot without picking his brain, cause if you get to know his heart, you've practically gotten to know the man.

Forever

The day you walked into my life, is the day my life changed, took a
turn for the better, the day we joined hands.

Caught by surprise, you and I were never planned, but I have no
regrets, because I would do it all over again.

I owe it to you, for being the man I am, you took a teenage boy and
converted him into a man.

Our love has no limit and that goes without saying, I meant forever
when I said forever, it's not a game that I'm playing.

Everyday won't be sunny and that I understand, but if we just pull
together, maybe we can find shelter when it rains.

Please forgive me, for every time I caused you pain, in my heart I
know that you love me, but as a man, sometimes that can be
hard to comprehend in the brain.

How is it possible, I have really nothing to offer but so much to gain,
if someone ask me why you love me, I couldn't possibly explain.

So, thank you for loving me and giving all you have, may God bless
our marriage, and may forever that it last.

Black and White

Black and White, two different colors, the only real difference is, one's a little darker than the other.

The blood we shed, makes us all sisters and brothers, we all bleed red, despite the difference in colors.

We deal with the same problems, same troubles, every day is a struggle, this senseless drama about color, just adds on to the stress and all the pressure we under.

We need to show respect and try our best to be humble, nobody chose to be who they are, it's just the way the ball bounced, the way the cookie crumbled.

Appreciate who you are and the race you came from, we not caged animals, neither are we roaming free in the jungle.

So, when it comes to color, I don't just see black or white, I see another human being living an innocent life.

What Is

What is life without humanity, humanity without sanity, what are
relatives without family, if everything is meaningless, then life
is just vanity.

What is love without trust, trust without love, what is the world
without the people and the people without the world.

What is believing without faith, faith without believing, when should
you give back, when should you be receiving.

What is fair and not fair, or sharing without share, how can you be
caring without care, it's like breathing without air, or depending
on someone that's not there.

What are your feelings without emotions, emotions without feel-
ings, it's like murder without killing, or having a cure that's not
healing.

What is living without dying, or happiness without crying, it's like
wanting success without trying, or being dishonest without
lying.

We can go on for years asking what is, but we can't have one without
the other and expect to still live.

Save A Life

Simply put, the choice is yours, you can pull the trigger, but you
   better know what's lying behind those doors.
You better be aware of the lines you'll cross, like time, you can never
   get back a life that's lost.
I wonder what can drive a person's mind off course, having them
   feeling like their hands are forced, having them willing to kill
   with no remorse.
That concept shouldn't even enter your thoughts, let alone, that's a
   feeling that shouldn't even enter your heart.
And if you're thinking straight, you should know that there's a better
   way to settle your differences without expressing your hate.
So do the world and yourself a favor, put the guns away and try to
   save a life today.

Still with Me

No matter where I go or how much time pass, my heart, my soul,
and my love for you, will forever last.

Forever now, forever more, in this life and the next, I'll be forever
yours.

Regardless of what world or planet I explore, if not here on earth, my
love a be waiting at heaven doors.

Only heaven knows, how my love continues to grow, you're the hope
and inspiration I'm living for.

With or without me, I think you should know, I'll love you forever
and wherever I go.

Confessions, confessions, out of my heart I pour, constantly express-
ing my love, until I can't no more.

And that's not only for now, but even when death do us part, you're
still be with me, cause not even death can stripe me of the love
I feel for you, forever in my heart.

Endless Pain

At a loss for words, I observe as she cries and weep, for the pain she feels, her lost, her grief.

Time like these, a person can be hard to reach, not knowing what to say, can make it harder to speak.

I listen carefully, as the preacher tries to preach, but the lesson to be learn, no man can teach.

Losing a child, is such a horrible grief, it pierces through the soul, that's buried beneath.

As she witnesses her child eternally sleep, her heart turns to stone and her pain increase.

There's no easy way to cope or find relief, but through the grace of God, the only grantor of peace.

So, judge this according to your own beliefs, but the world as we know, to her has become decease.

Mi Truth…
|_OV£|_!£€

TONI BURGESS

Mi Truth

This is Mi Truth it's not necessarily for you;
stick around if you care to.

Know that this journal was created with my
experiences and point of view.

Some inspired by some of you;
others just straight out of the blue.

No copywriter, that's true;
because I have a love of life to share with you.

In this day and age some have not a clue;
of God's presence inside of you.

So, speak up loud and true;
you'll never know the impact that shines from within you.

Thank you to a special two;
you've awakened something I use to do.

Uvie and Geo, I will always love you.

All Aboard

"The making Toni happy train" has been traveling these railroads of life for many years. Its transportation of precious cargo and passengers from different parts and walks of life is not what makes it unique. Rather, it's the sincerity of her all-aboard call that gives every individual the distinct opportunity to experience an irreplaceable personality that whistles through each destination with the steam powered locomotive delivered by God's love, grace, and mercy.

The baggage stored within her core is admitted not only by its passengers but is collected with the conductors' very own spirited wear. Baggage left by travelers of the past and present gives the cargo carriage an expansive sprung into reality these days.

Unlike in her heydays, left alone, the singular railcar searched the rails for miles to find other railway trains to attach to as she toured in unfamiliar territories. Blessed with other conductors who would take stance alongside her while traveling the simplest to the hardiest railways of her continued lifespan.

Now, that the tracks have shifted, and the operations and maintenance of her old soul matures. She is no longer in search and is kept by the angels who fly above her and saved by some of the rarest second, third, and forth locomotives who is permanently and/or semi-permanently attached or the temporary who has been placed on a shared track just to assist her up steep banks or to provide braking power on her way down.

Knowing that the supervision of her future, security, passengers, and cargo is the responsibility of the conductor. She is fixed to a schedule commenced by high speeds at times. The "Stop this Train" button that interlines her very existence and that triggers a pain through her engine is always present to those whom choose it. She also occupies the right to discard cargo or passengers that threaten a toxic pollution upon her and the love, peace, and happiness that dwell within each of those who choose to accompany her on her journey.

Enjoying the new scenery of life and expanding on her machinery currently "The making Toni happy train" is running at expected capacity levels and after a few adjustments she'll be traveling "full speed ahead" once again "All-Aboard".

Burning Bridges

You burnt the bridge;
    I gave you a yacht.

You crashed the yacht;
    I provided you with a boat.

You sunk the boat;
    I returned with a kayak.

You capsized the kayak;
    I sent out the Coast Guard.

But all they could find was a shell of a man… Unidentifiable!

Book Shop

ONE
SIDED
STORIES
NEVER
COME
OFF
THE
FICTION
AISLE

A Portrait in Oil

you painted a canvas
you let it sit and dry
you hung it up
before their eyes
to take it down
would mean you lied
now no one can ever
know the truth inside

Famished

I'm starving for you
but my appetite is gone
I won't eat anything else
so, I have no brawn
the fluids in me
are not enough
to keep me strong
I'm starving for you
but my taste buds say you're wrong
the seasoning is off
and you're tougher than fawn
my hearts at risk
from calories gone
my muscles are thin
and my veins are withdrawn
I'm starving for you
afraid they'll find my corpses on the front lawn.

Speechless

Fumble your strengths;
Live in your flaws;
Believe in your failures;
Strive through your accomplishments;
Challenge your freedom;
Embrace your enemies;
Focus on your shortcomings;
Relish in the ability to see the what if's, how comes, shouldn't haves, and never again's.
Then close your eyes and breath knowing that life happens and then you live.

Planted Not Buried

Color me yellow; Color me blue;
In lightness or darkness;
Grace is upon you.

Grant me the strength of thee;
Give me serenity;
In all things that abideth within me;
Or set me free.

Neither cold nor hot;
Lukewarm is what I've got.

Let your palms sweat not;
For God hasn't forgot.

Reverse thy roll;
Stand where I uphold;
See Mi Truth;
Know that I Love you.

Search my soul;
Search my heart;
Never will they part;

God blessed me from the start.

Back and forward we go;
Why? Only you know.
Each seed that I sow;
God blossoms as it grows.

Correct thy wrong;
Violins, you aren't needed for this song.
Sing it from within the soul;
hearts don't need burying; in holes.

Six Word Story #1

Love multiplies; it cannot be divided.

Today I Will...

She's my friend.
Honestly, she is...

At least for today that is.

She comprehends my thoughts.
For real, she hears me talk...

At least for today that is.

She makes me laugh
Genuinely, almost wetting her pants...

At least for today that is.

She senses my affliction.
No kidding, she reaches for the pain...

At least for today that is.

She seizes my tears.
Seriously, she wipes each drop...

At least for today that is.

Who is she?
Is she me?

At least for today that is.

No Vacancy

love lives here
yes, in me
opens its eyes
seeing things clearly

pain lives here
yes, in me
singing the sour songs
of sweet melodies

fear use to reside
a few doors away
now that you're here
I haven't seen its face

hope moved in
on the other side
right next to my heartbeat

God's Cry

Welling up as a mighty ocean;

Pouring out like a river;

Flowing down the narrowest creek;

Seeping in at the mouth of its stream;

Evaporating upon the heart of the earth's core; is...

God's tear upon the face of the earth.

Sweet Kiss

Cover me with your soft lips
place hands upon my hips
lay your brow
against my heart's breath
rest your tongue
against the walls
of engraved happiness.

Market Value

no one to charge
for we are the product of our decisions
a sales pitch of our transgressions
a name branded within our beliefs
a testimony before our Judge
that created all bills
refunded by His resurrection
once He was bargained for
the convictions of our greed

Six World
Story #2

"When nothing adds up… Stop Counting!"

Judge Oneself

Roll out the red carpet for me. I'm walking in places you wouldn't
believe, places you cannot see. Coming around corners of disbe-
lief taking paths meant for me. That's right, it's what it's gonna
be… All About Me!

If you can't handle it take a guilty plea and sentence yourself away
from me. No time for a lifelong incarceration with thee. I live to
be free my soul rises above the judgement of anybody.

I got me, as long as I keep my faith in, He the judge of that which is
within me.

A Gun to The Head

From the cradle to the grave… don't be raised
by a system designed to enslave.

"Life without the possibility" a phrase;
putting you in the state of captivity;
numbing your flexibility.
Rise above the bars and the chains,
be the picture that frames this game.

Hang amongst the "Justice of the Peace…"
knowing that you're a part of His masterpiece.
With that bow and arrow aimed at the back of your head;
no one is watching… for the Bull's Eye is Red.
It only takes one eye to see; the second is to better visibility.

Enough

I'm not tall or short...
Enough
My skin isn't shaded or pale...
Enough
These hips aren't shapely or slender...
Enough
Well, at least the length of my hair has no bearing; it's just? ...
Enough
The thickness of my lips aren't silent and don't cry out...
Enough
So, go ahead... look at me because I am...
Enough

Whisperz in the Dark

When I'm gone talk to me.
Even whispers can be heard in the dark and dirt can't muffle the
spirit.
That prayer that was whispered over me that day was a formality;
that's why you couldn't hear it.
      I wish, I could turn back time.
      I wish, the dead could be brought back.
      I wish, I couldn't hear your whispers amongst the silence.
   The expected wouldn't be so scary if these things were possible.
Death by caliginosity is always preventable.
No one is born with the desire to die in the whispers of darkness.

      How does it happen?
      One day you can hear, see, and feel eternity;
      then the darkness threatens to eliminate it; take it all back.
The constant criticism and lack of affection should of did the job
but some minds are stronger than most.
Now that the eyes become dilated and each shallow breath brushes
across the cheek
like a whisper in the dark;

      who's the blame?
      Was it Trust?
Maybe, it was the respect of it all or could it have been the belief
in it all.
Love, is that a light at the end of the tunnel; I see?
Did the beginning come before the end or was it always the end?

      Did others see it first?
Was it wrong for them to believe that it was darkness all along or is
it because they all live in the dark and that's all they know; so that's
all they see?

Whispered lies to themselves in the darkness deflecting any possibility of trust, respect, belief, or love.

Who remembers the beginning anyway?
That moment that the light flickers through. In order for anyone to remember that moment
they would have to remember the whispers of darkness before it. The shadow of possibilities between each breath reveals something about that time;
but it's too dark for reflection.

Born out of darkness into a radiant energy that promises a return to a darken whisper…

… go ahead and whisper it already!

The words that no one is ever ready for but is born to expect…

… ""Shh! goodbye."

Mother; Dearest to Me

If you can't hear her; hear me!!!
I speak her words all through me.
Look into my eyes if you dare to see;
her strength that glows from within me.
Yes, I was made in his image as you can see;
but I came out of her and she lives within me.
Showing how she feels comes naturally;
because she is my mom a true beauty;
hurt her and you will deal with me.
Because she is the solider and I her shield;
you best believe.

I Cry Too

I have a tear for you.
The kind that I've always knew would
come and blind my view of you.
The kind that flows from deep inside of you.
I have a few stored up in the eyelids of my point of view.
But I chose this one for you.
See its special too, it's been awaiting that perfect moment
to spew out into the worlds view. Those whom have a clue
knows that it took two to create this tear coming through.
Welling up in the corner of my life's hue is
the tear that God created for you.
Trying to hold it back won't do.
The purpose of it is to cleanse my soul's view.
"Cry me a river" ok, and if I do…
will you then allow me to see You?

It's Love

I thought about it.
I closed my eyes and envisioned it.
I laid myself down and played it over and over in my head.
I let it breath through the vessels of my heart, body, and soul.
I tasted the flavorful diversity of its kind and I'm sure, I'm positive,
I'm convinced…
It's love.

The High Road

... a road paved
with new scenery
untraveled scenes
of a new historical plea

... "Ass-phalt" of tar
turning the travail
of pass potholes
you didn't see
the other drivers
who cut you off?
in agony
aggressively, excelling
the speed limits
of their journey

... this road trip ahead
is for me
change in the world
surrounding me
across miles throughout
this spiritual journey
shifting the direction of me
while the streetlight's glow
inside of this love
that's traveling through me

... change in the spinning
of the wheel that
JESUS
holds for me
with the expectation
of the red lights

that will stop me
the anticipated
yield sign
A WARNING
to pay attention
to the streets ahead
of my destiny

Six Word Story #3

Words Behind Walls They Do See

Incarcerated

It's a crime to have to do my time like this; sitting in your abyss
of my destruction. I don't have enough fingers to point at a
cause, the cause, you caused, the whispers of charged eruptions.
Imprisoned, on your offense of internal, eternal, the infernal
inhabitant of interruption. Misdemeanor acts of affection tugging
at invisible strings of your evil and corruption. Rap sheets attesting
the truth of my transgression; a bad rap for a love in the wrong
direction. A never-ending sentence to a wicked extraction where
self is just a reflection of reformatory depression. Gazing at this
stockade impression, embedding my hopes in each session used
for the repossession of my intimate confessions like a high-priested
bully session. Unjust in your oppression, clinging onto family
connections that I alone… put under suppression, relieving me of
aggression while I sit in this big house for our vanished progression.
I send up an intercession on my knees behind
these walls of decompression.

A Gift That Came Alive

You're more than an image…a vision…a force…a
prophesy come true; one that was long overdue.

The look in your eyes mesmerized my heart; your spirit hypnotized
me from the start. Passion, so sweet never tart. No fantasized
thought; just pure love play's this part. As I look at you, I feel, not
see… it fills up all with inside of me. Covering me from head-
to-toe is your love that continues to grow. Shielding every part of
me is your vision not image of me; the force of His prophesy.

Mesmerized, hypnotized, no never fantasized…is His love pure
as the river that cries through these eyes and that plays the only
part worth playing in our lives. That's why this love can rise and
thrive making it through whatever that arrives. You and I are the
perfect size wrapped up like a surprise only for us to realize.
A Gift That Came Alive

The Eagle Soars

Soaring over the tree tops,
lifting souls to be groomed and cropped to represent thy flock.
Soldier, you can't be stopped.
One-hundred together "Let's Rock".
"Ninety-nine and a half won't do" on my clock.
Don't worry bout me just a quick pit stop;
be back before the clouds drop;
having a little prayer with pops.
Flying over the moon and through the stars,
capturing each universe; collided with Mars.
Passing the sun, burning thy sins away,
Angels melting thy heart before the winds carry me back your way.

Perfection of Assumption

Your perception is just that… your perception an
opinion, a conception, a religion-based notion, a
visionary lesson taught by your aggressions or lack
of compassion. Judging nothing but a ration
of the truth… Mi Truth. Take the section that is best for
your digestion and get past the brief digression because
you don't control my passion, you don't see my actions…
words sum up your life long lessons. The spirit takes the
lead in this precession guided by His reflection.

Dressed Within the Naked Truth

A woman with a naked eye sees you as a man wearing nothing at all. She allows you to pick out your own cloth. She waits for each stitch to be sown. She skillfully helps you pick out the buttons, the cuffs, all of the unique accessories that matches your persuaded personality. Once cleaned and pressed she hangs this outfit inside your perceptive wardrobe.

When asked to dress you she pulls out this worn and sometimes soiled outfit that you so consciously modeled before her naked eye. Respectfully, no matter how many times you undress before her or how many outfits comes about, she'll never see you naked again.

Six Word
Story #4

"If you want happiness, Make It!"

Death by Time

They got me in a death trap; not knowing that faith sustains me. Time cannot be stopped; it refines me. Like the clock, my love ticks' pastimes away. Like a perennial each season replaced by the reincarnation of my rejuvenate love. Levels of maturity taking root; surpassing the soil that once buried it. Pounded like a yam from all directions. I rise; as He did on the third day with serpents taking their last breath at the foot of my tomb.

My guardian angel whose birthright has been appointed to me. Tattered wings and a breastplate of gold protecting the purest heart; matching the perfectly flawed Son of God. Thy fraternal twin.

Displayed Anger

Look at your face, your tone…
… and I'm not talking about your race.
Even your posture is out of place.
Teeth clinched, suffocated by the lack of air in this space.
Amazed by how your coming together with others can cause such
a dramatic change in our pace. Damn, we're basically standing
in place. Letting other condemnations shred us like lace.
You can't even look at the one you're supposed to love; in the
face. A guilty conscious for your love agape… its only desire is to
escape the chains that you let others put in your hearts place.
I'm not worried for it's a journey; not a race.
Invested with a currency of love;
not hidden agendas or anger misplaced.
No one has ever tried to stop you from running in place,
because they know it keeps you in their grace, no matter
the displayed anger shown… right in their face.

Displayed Anger II

Your heart might as well be a game of
Cut & Paste for those who compete for first place.
Seemingly, unnecessary competition amongst
those who share your birthplace.
Those that already hold the ace of hearts; in the first place. A bloodline
that can't be erased by anything or anyone just their self-inflicted
deface; constantly fighting over what they already have… "A Place".
Unknowingly or knowingly, placing each link around your hearts
embrace. Leaving those of us who dare to come face-to-face with hope
that has already been replaced by insecurities of another's face. Paralyzing
the love once it's in place, marrying it to a sub space behind the chains
of your hearts showcase. But like I said… this is a journey, not a race. I
know that God will guide you to your rightful place and I'll stand beside
you until that displayed anger turns into the image of God's grace.

Displayed Anger III

Who are we to judge another's holy place?
Gods loving grace that rest upon our embrace.
Our beliefs shouldn't chase behind the human race. Acceptance of others isn't
necessary to Him it's a disgrace that can land the soul in an open fireplace.
Serving Him is what gets you to a higher place. No need for that poker face;
He knows your heart in any case. Be slow to anger if you want to touch base
with Gods embrace. Do right by those He put in place to avoid living in a
null space. Understanding His guidance will take place in your heart; not
cyberspace. Forgiving of self is what allows forgiveness of others to take place.
Those who have the knowledge base can speak with a straight face… and
no, they don't need a memory trace. The truth is like a clocks face; it has
moving parts but time passing doesn't mean it gets a reface. To get the best
out of this human race remove that displayed anger on your face, get out of
your own way, and let the purest form of God in you be your showplace.

Displayed Anger IV

If you can't see it through stay in place,
let love free your mind and direct you to His commonplace.
Love leaves no aftertaste, no empty space, it can beat afterlife in the
broken hearts place. If there's anything in life that deserves a high-
speed chase; it's love… the purest image of God's grace. When love
is driven by anything but love its driving towards a deaden space.
When love lives through you it can't be erased, misplaced, or ignored
in any case; it will always stay in place. Love cannot fail so when
you think it's gone away it's your lack of faith that's been misplaced;
either by self or others pulling you into agony and disgrace channeling
the anger and hurt you've deeply store in an unsafe place. Why does
love stay? We chase, but seemingly It gets away. Love doesn't get
away. It may lie dormant while waiting for you to pick up the pace.
If you believe, it will fill up every space and show its face. Love is
like a paste holding everything in place, embrace it within faith to
keep it safe from life's toxic waste. Love doesn't crave a regimental
taste, nor does it see boundaries you put in place, it lives beyond
anyone's imaginary showcase and interface directly with Gods
harmonizing grace removing all displayed anger upon your face.

Goodnight

Holding on for dear life
as I go through this fight
the thought of taking flight
it's reducing my might
to write out the mental plight
playing through my hearts sight

If I could, if I might
be so lucky to be right
about our love, our life
a dream that I've dreamed every night
since you came into my sights
dreams do come true, right

Why do you start these fight's?
to see if my love will take flight
to test the theory of who's right
meanwhile night by night
my dream makes it alright

You do realize that one night
it's gonna be my last night
and you're going to have to live
with that day before fight

Blindsided

One step at a time Jack, walking backwards in pitch black, intoxicated by the flak in your voice never keeping intact, pushing back intelligence enduring the lack of common sense on the minds rack, closing in on the paperback style rap communicated to set a trap planning out a personal attack, risking a smack like we did in Iraq, in this mental shack comes an atomic weapon drawback, unpacked from the best thwack thrown aback is the yolk sac keeping the heart from its natural react to bounce back from the clack created by the act of two spirits wrecked.

Bleeding Heart

I always knew she would be hurt.
I always knew she would see the best in me and grow me like weeds beneath a willow tree while watering these roots of empathy so that my emotions hang lower than the branches around me. Like a predictor I preyed on her like the seeds planted before me. There was something about her blossom that drew out a growth spurt within the grounded roots you see. Safely tucked away from everything but me she cries rivers for me; literally… without her nectar I would be thirsty. She's the bleeding heart that's being uprooted by me.

Six Word Story #5

All of your nothings; are something.

I Huffed and I Puffed

A fly on the wall desperately trying not to fall from the
crash of reality being thrown in the hall… The elephant
in that room maybe well-groomed but I'd rather be
outside looking at the cow jump over the moon…
Watching you count sheep instead of getting a good
night sleep is for the birds; angry birds you creep…
Lions, tigers, and bears oh my; they all look sacred for the
boy sitting on his bed crying wolf… while the wolf huffed
and puffed and blew down the whole fucking house.

I Can't Swim

I want to cry.
I want to shed more tears than I have inside of me.
I want this pain to dampen my dried-out heart.
I want the anger to flow through my arteries so that these veins can
refill my heart with the parts of me that makes you the happiest.
Allowing streams of laughter and love to overflow the mental
downpour of sorrow. Revive our collapsed spirits with waterfalls
of joy and peace. Trying to hold in the moisture produced by
the emotional anguish felt throughout this emptied vessel is
overwhelming to say the least. Trying to row without a paddle in
sight instead becoming a bogy weighted down by the anxiety and
fear of losing your interest, respect and most of all your love. I've
learned so much from loving you why didn't you teach me to swim?
Don't you get it?
If you take your life jacket away, I will
vanish beneath this sea of tears.

Just One Look And...

His bottom lip disappeared, the room cleared, and it was now just
the two of us, sharing a cocktail of passion with a twist of lust.

Trying not to be seen by those we no longer see, while his
eyes reveal the deepest parts of me; capturing full glimpses
of the insides of me. Confident in his ability; making me
feel everything he sees; he never took his eyes off me.

My body responded instantly, there wasn't a second to count
before he was inside of me. No, not metaphorically. In my
mind, this was factually. Even though, there was no other
who could collaborate this story with me; other than he.

Just one look and... he created a mystery; for some, but not for
me. My eyes were opened as wide as they could ever be, and it
was clear that he was still in love with me. More determined
than he'd ever be, to make that second last for an eternity.

This may not sound sexy, but his ankles pressed up against
mine took away our gravity. I thought that the rise in his
jeans would float him away from me but the gravitational
force between my legs held him right there, inside of me.

Changing our position, his eyes I could no longer see.
Yet, I felt them all over me and the sound of his voice
asking me to place pressure on his anatomy took away
the breath that he had just put inside of me.

Respecting our privacy, he spun me around so that no
one would see him partake in what was now our reality.
Flesh-to-flesh... Soft and firm he held it perfectly. Placing
each finger, oh-so-softly around his half-moon fancy.

Satisfied as I could be, knowing that a mouthful
and a handful was all he would need, any more than
that could be called the third sin; Greed.

There is no ending to this story no matter what others
professed to see; he never stopped looking at me. And those
hands… Yes, those hands, they're still holding onto me.

No Other Man Can

The world in the palm of my hand; no other man can.
Although it's slippery when wet, thy grip protects those who let the
tongue confess and the knee progress towards He who will bless.
In the beginning was the end.... and it is still
holding on as strong as your best friend.
No saint to uphold... the soul of the sinner has been sold...
"bad-to-the-bone" breeds weakness; if truth be told.
Thy good and faithful servant conquers,
for in my image... he; I mold.
The price is right and with all my might I will take flight
releasing you from the darkness; bringing you to light.
The pits of hell will no longer beam in your sight.
Fire and brimstone won't keep me away from
the palm of my hand; no other man can.

Happy Birthday

Every year that passes by
I wish for another that I will stay alive
being as happy as the kid inside

Every year I learn a little more
about this life that I endure;
I let that kid out even more
as I find the happiness that I am striving for

Every year I try to even the score
and some years I come out a little sore
from the battles suffered the year before,
being that kid gets harder as I grow more and more

Every year I give what I stand for
while answering the question of "what for?"
that, that kid is accounted for

Today dawns like the years before
another year of loving you even more
for being that kid who I stand for
giving the happiness to continue to explore
while being this grown-up heretofore

Happy Birthday to the kid, I adore and to the soul I live for

World Class Athlete

… you're my up and down

that which is in the middle

and that which comes around

the axle in which my world spins around

located at the top, your crown

situated at the bottom, my solid ground

throughout the center, I've found

the core of my hearts pounding sound

rhythmical beating, I'm astounded

at the love propound, we've come so far now

eternally ready for the subsequent rebound

from whatsoever players around, our compound

passionately keeping our affection inbound

turning those frowns upside down like the class clown

forces rebound within the desire, unbound

building the reflecting heart sound

spinning around the hub of the coordinates

He put down.

Morn'ting...

Good Morning Sunshine.
Today is bright and full of peace.
The warmth of your spirit woke me.
Outside, the trickle of your tears arise like rabbit ears on me.
The night was calm the willow slept...
gently, resting its limbs upon me.
Nestled between your thighs was the portions of me.
Cuddled in your neck was the breath I breathe.
Good Morning Sunshine.
The first day's difficulty... is getting up out
of this bed to go make your coffee.

The End of Time

The earth will spin, the sun will shine, the moon will glow, the star will show...

No matter the season, the-day, eve-of-the-day, the-day past.
Each instant is given; without your control. Be grateful for the time...

The seconds looking into each other's eyes, the moments our souls rise, the minutes kissing, the hours holding, the days missed, the weeks of bliss, the months of... "I Yours ~ Your Mine." Throughout, these years of pure love divine.

Time given to you, time given to me, one-plus-one truly equals three; for its God's grace and will that get us through the generations ahead you see.

"The End" ...No, that could never be.

Magic Trick

Between a rock, a hard place.
Get out of my space.
Give me room to run this race.
Take that smile off your face.
I'm still in first place.

There's no room for gloom out in space just the stars
join me in this drag race. With God conducting, I
don't need my shoes laced… to keep the pace.

You try to trace my steps and take my grace?
No worries, cause I'm the original… I can't be replaced.
Ride or die with angels that cry; crystal tears run from these eyes.
Sniffs of love is how I get by.
Filling my heart up to the sky with faith and trusting no lie.

Like a warrior, if I should die my spirit will be left
to help "the-one" get by… and if he dies; his spirit
will cry… "We Are Never Saying Goodbye."

Ta dumb ta dumb.

Speak Now or Forever...

I hear you talking to me
but it's not your breath behind those words
that's a harsh pant I hear
it's a gasp of disbelief
hot air winds of chatter
flutter of what never matters
whiffs of fear
puffs near my ear
sigh of guilt
talking within disguised vocal cords
speak now or forever lose your voice

Thank you, Lord...

Upon this rock, I stand with my arms open wide.
Let know evil collide upon me; for it's your word I see.
Grant me the serenity and continue to guide me.
Call my name each day let my tears fall upon thee.
Let my soul live free.
Shower your love while I bend my knee; giving all the glory to thee.
Thanking you for those who can see; the spirit of you in me.
Help those who have jealousy in their heart for me.
Please Lord, give them peace and set them free.
Thank you for momma's prayers for me.
Thank you for the man who stands beside me.
Thank you for the child you've given me.
Yesterday has left me and today I am free.
Thank you, Lord for I am Me.

London Life

LEONARD LONDON JR.

Lenx

Was she faithful? Did she love me?
Who was that person behind the iron curtain?
Rose colored glasses for good ole Len, that much for certain
Perhaps unfaithfulness is approved, "In God We Trust"
Why not bust the monotony, divorce is a must?
I'll just keep on trucking and bask in the Son
Hello? I have the answers to my questions now…. You're welcome

My Son

Separated at birth but reunited later
Against all odds nothing could fade us
My pride and joy and the apple of my eye
The bond we share shall never die
In this life things will never be perfect
So, we must learn to love deep and well below the surface
You are my greatest gift from God, and I will always treasure
My love for you is too much for measure

Someone Special

My dearest friend, so wild and free
Your spirit runs rampant, no naked eye can see
We started out casual and without desire for more
But God stepped in and revealed what He had in store
Your beautiful smile and alluring conversation
You have a unique gift for enhancing relations
I often wondered what you were up to
But He knew best and carried it through
In the process I became a better man
Open up Leonard and rely on His plan

Ponchatoula, La.

At age 6 is when we met
The day I first laid eyes, I'll never forget
Your quiet charm and peaceful demeanor
Embedded in my soul like a butcher's cleaver
On good days and bad, I've basked in your glory
You have firsthand account and can attest to my story
No matter where this life takes me or where I may roam
You will always be the place that I call home

In the Heat

This will be a good day
That's what I always say
Today for certain because we go to the house to pray
All appears well if viewing from afar
Pretty suits, smiling faces, and look, someone has the most expensive car
At further glance and after the facade is over
There lies a little boy asleep with a four-leaf clover
Is God still here? Can I make a wish?
Please don't allow the day to go amiss
And then it happens, in the heat of the night
The sound of two Christians in a heated fight
What should I do? Is this my fault?
What happened to the people that took a vow to love at all cost?
But it doesn't matter because I'm used to it now
I'll just tune it out the best way I know how
Problem solved and all is well on the surface
But wait, who am I? What is love? What is my purpose?

Brother J

JJ Lathers, there will never be another
Legally we are cousins, but it felt like brothers
We used to clown as kids play fighting and wrestling
Those were the best of times, carefree and enjoying God's blessing
As young men, we did our thing
Riding around bumping Tupac, starched, iron and clean
The ladies used to halt traffic to get a better view
Mostly because of brother J but I managed to pull a few
You did everything first and I saw you take your bride at 16
Some may have said too young, but God knew how much longer you
    had on the scene
You lived rugged and raw and other's opinions did not matter
When it came time to take your lick, your response was simply
    "You're looking for me, I'm Jonathan Lathers"
They put you in time-out and everyone thought you were through
I still remember those late-night calls, "Cuz, I need you""
When you got free, your smile lit up the place
We dapped, hugged and shared a warm embrace
"Cuz, lets chill at the cafe, I'll buy us a case of beer"
You were definitely a badass, but your love was always sincere
We hung out for hours, shooting pool and confessing
Life would soon teach one of its greatest lessons
We crossed paths one last time by chance in the mall
You were looking for all-black air-max for your late-night Ball
Several hours late, I got the news
Cuz put up a fight but was outnumbered by a crew
You did everything first and now your home
Until we meet again, rest in peace and I love you Jonathan Jerome

Church

Sing, sing, sing
Talk, talk, talk
If I don't make it into heaven, it's this church's fault
So many activities to merely scratch the surface
But you know what they say, "no church is perfect"
The condition of the heart, that's what the Word says
I wonder why this is overshadowed by what appears to be show biz
Money, Money, Money
Give, Give, Give
Salvation is free
But the" church" needs this to live
So, by and by we go through the motions
Then hope and pray for a special potion
Maybe one day we can get back to God's plan from the start
Truth, actions and the condition of the heart

Nature Retreat

I have a lot on my mind and need to release
It's time for a walk to set my mind at ease
The gym is near but before I embark
I think I'll make my way to the nearest park
Such beautiful scenery as I look around
Trees, a pond, and the well-groomed grounds
Squirrels at play without a care in the world
Parents in the playground with the little boys and girls
The ambience of nature attacks as I take my scroll
It transcends my spirit and heals my soul
All is well in the world right now
A trip to the park, my daily vow

Quiet

A world of my own
A world I call home
Others celebrate in revelry
I prefer to be alone
I enjoy the love from gatherings with genuine family and friends
But after a flash, I prefer to be by myself again
Inner peace is my paradise and I have to sustain
Talk is cheap but actions remain
The world is full of endless chatter
I'm programmed to think deeply and upon things that matter
I used to feel guilty about my disposition and tried to appease
That's no longer the case... silence please

Small Talk

I'm blessed with kindness
Although it may not appear
Because I do not smile & chat
When a stranger is near
My foundation is truth
And persona is genuine
It comes out when interacting with a close friend
Much talk can be a covert weapon
The words of some can cause a person to become undone
We're all a part of the same body
This much I do agree
But until I get to know you
Let's keep it short and sweet

Ant

I'll never forget the moment I first saw you
Barely walking yet your soul shined though
Time marches on and now you're a man
But I'll forget the time you took a dump in a trash can
I assisted in your upbringing
And that gave me much pleasure
Even in the midst of a storm
Life reveals its greatest treasures
God works in mysterious ways and this trumps our plans
We have to learn to submit our will
And leave it in His hands
You've always had a good heart, don't ever change
Your journey will not be perfect
But let your character remain
Love you Big Ant, you will always be dear to me
Stay positive, achieve your goals
And let the world see the person I know you to be

Family

Mom, Dad, Son, Brothers
My family is unique and like no other
Grandson, nieces, nephews, friends
I vow unconditional love until the end
Aunts, uncles, and cousins including those removed
We may not see each other often but our bond is approved
We celebrate together when good news is received
And uplift one another when the family is grieved
Special events, holidays, or a simple walk in the park
Love from family resonates and adds a special spark
It's a blessing to share with those that care about your overall well-being
A warm embrace and friendly face are all that matters in the end
Treasure family as I do, you'll be happy you did
Material matters come and go but love from family can never be rid

Integrity

Hidden motives in this crazy world
Lack of integrity and deceit unfurled
An honest handshake and word as bond
Lost in the wind and traded for stardom
Show me a place where integrity matters
And I'll show you a place where the land is fatter
Come one, come all to this special place
Everyone is genuine- no need to hide face
But it's all just fantasies because of our current state
A man can dream though, who else can relate?
In the interim, I'll keep on hoping and praying
And do my part to make this a better place to stay in
Not just for current generation, but for all my seeds
Because they deserve to live in a place where integrity is lead

Basketball

I fell in love with the game and it was never the same
Up at the crack of dawn practicing my skills down the lane
Swish…there it is, another 3-point shot
And yet another one, this time pretending there's a game clock
On and on until the sun gives in
After I eat, shower and sleep, I'm back at it again
All summer long this was my routine
My goal was to dribble like Magic and Skyhook like Kareem
Folks from all over town knew of my court
They'd come to compare skills and run a game of some sort
Eventually I played on my junior high team
My skills were solid, but my frame was lean
In high school I applied the same intensity
Ole coach told me I was too short, and basketball wasn't meant for me
The following year I grew a couple of inches
I did not try out because I somewhat lost interest
Same ole coach saw me hooping in the school gym and tried to recruit
But it was too late by then, stubbornness had taken root.
Oh, you want me to know, I was the same player last year
I don't get down like that, but I'll lend you my ear
"What about the cheerleaders and popularity status?"
"With skills like yours, you'd definitely be one of the baddest"
Thank you, sir it's an honor indeed
But I prefer to focus on my studies and education to succeed
I still loved the game and played as often as possible
I became one of the best and my shot was unstoppable
Father time has visited but I'm still not too shabby
Try me if you want and I'll have you calling me daddy
Engrained in my system with no remorse
Basketball will forever be my favorite sport

Dan and Don

Dan and Don, the London family's favorite sons
Twin is what they called them
But I called them cousins
Suave and charismatic since the days I can remember
Easy on the eyes and could pull any girl's number
They stayed with us during vacations and we were the London clan
I looked up to my cousins, I was their biggest fan
As they got older the streets called their name
I would still see them, but I could tell things had changed
Bonafide outlaws and they had no fear
They would soon pay the ultimate price and lessen their years
Dan left us at 29 which stole everyone's joy
His last words to me were "Hey, I love you boy"
Don did a bid but is now roaming free
I'm proud of big Cuz, he's now living positively
After it's all said and done my cousins were a blessing
I'll always cherish and love them, this is my confession
Dan and Don always in my heart

A Friend

The word is misused; does anyone know what it means?
Seems like nowadays it's measured by data on a computer screen
Take me back to the old school when the fellowship was real
Even in a fight, the bond is only sealed
Through thick and thin, a true friend has your back
Most "friendships" are rooted in selfishness now and that's a fact
A true friend is a blessing from God and must be treated as such
A friendship ordained by Him is holy and cannot be touched
How many can we call a true friend, can anyone answer?
Take time to evaluate, don't respond on a whim
If it so happens your answer is miniscule
Reset your priorities and focus on friendships that are true

Solitude

I meditate, I reflect, I quiet my mind
In such moments, I'm hard to find
I sleep, I rest, and I ponder my thoughts
These times are precious and could never be bought
I walk, I run, I perform daily tasks
The experience is pure, and results unmasked
My spirit is nourished, in the end is peace
My body is relaxed, and my soul is at ease
Like a tree planted by the river, I cannot be moved
Keep the fame and attention, I prefer solitude

Free

No cares in the world, that's the place to be
No worries and no stress, yes, that's for me
Material items add value in proper perspective
But must not be traded for spiritual objectives
I'll take it all but not if it comes with a cost
Because I cannot allow my freedom to be lost

Schooling

K-12, yes, I'll play along
Every day it's the same ole song
Hip, Hip, Hip, Hop, Hooray
I'm gonna get some schooling today
Columbia discovered America, was this correct?
Will I ever need Algebra to write that check?
Some is needed to a certain degree
English, science, and true history
No mention of credit scores in the schooling I received
Life taught this lesson and it was a tough one indeed
Morals, integrity and self-respect
Not a class on these subjects but I digress
Teach 'em to memorize data. Was this the plan?
We'll make them little computers and less human
Test, test, test, to evaluate that knowledge
Is the playing field even or somewhat biased?
All in all, it's quite the experience
Hopefully one day we'll see a difference
Until that time, we'll forget the wrong
Obedience is mandatory so let's sing along
Hip, hip, hip hop hooray
I'm gonna get some schooling today

Braxton

July is our month and Friday is our day
We're bonded for eternity; I'll show you the way
London and Lathers blood run through our veins
We are all God's children, yet we are not the same
Education and discipline on one side of the clan
You'll find this helpful on the road to becoming a man
Bible and church also in this pool
But focus on relationship and not religious rules
Flip the coin and reverse the tide
You'll find strong qualities not likely to subside
Love is displayed in its purest form
Yet, some lifestyles are rogue and far from norm
They may not attend a church on a weekly basis
But they always have your back in moments of crisis
Free-spirited at core and entrepreneurial minded
Some run-ins with the law while working and grinding
All things considered, it's a pretty solid disposition
Embrace your truths and don't fret if you don't quite fit in
Sometimes staying true to self will come with sacrifice
May you always feel my love as you journey through life

When Real Meets Rude

I can see it, I can feel it, oh what a blessing
Lie to me if you want but I can feel it in your essence
Shall I reveal your truth and burst your bubble?
Or oblige the superficial event to alleviate trouble
Merrily, Merrily, Merrily, is this what you want?
Forgive me if I am unable to maintain this front
If I see the contrary in the words you express
I'll be brief to keep from doing something we'll regret
So, don't push the issue because things may get real
That would be rude of me, so we'll keep it concealed

Do You Need Me?

Hello, is anyone there? How are you today?
This is Leonard aka Lenny Len from around the way
I heard there was a party, and it turned out swell
Didn't get the invite but I hope all is well
What? She got married? How was the wedding?
I know we haven't spoken in a while, but I wouldn't have missed it
for anything
I know I'm partly the blame due to my introverted nature
But it's all love from me, that much for sure
Beep, Beep, now who could this be calling my line
"Hey Len, can you help me out this one last time?"
Knock, knock, now someone is calling at my door
"I know you've helped me in the past, can I bother you for more?"
"I made a mistake man and now I'm in trouble"
If it wasn't for such communication, my social life would be rubble
Maybe it's my destiny to live my life as such
I will not complain though and there's no need to fuss
So, to all my friends and family, if you need me, I'm here
Much love to everyone with positive vibes and cheer

G-Lyfe

Today was eventful, work was a beast
I'll make up for it by going home to feast
Not too much though, I prefer my physique slim
So, after I eat and relax, I need to hit the gym
Late night workouts are what I love
I have the gym to myself. Thanks, Man above!
Water-check, Earphones-check
I'm ready to get it in and give it my best
Start off on the treadmill and knock it out with ease
Next off to the bench press…add 250 please!
On and on until I feel my muscles jump
Then cool down on the Stairmaster until my body is pumped
As I scan the scene, everyone is getting it in
Taking care of their temple- no time for sin
Ladies looking lovely in the tanks and leggings
I would try to holla, but I don't want to lose my blessings
Work-out complete and I'm out the door
See you tomorrow G-Lyfe, I'll be back for more

Behind the Screen

Escape from reality that would be great!
It's been a long week; I want to hide my face
Much to do but no time for stressing
Forget this adulthood and harsh life lessons
Maybe I'll take a peek at the life of others
I wonder what a trip to the movies uncovers
Bright lights, cozy seats and the awesome screen
You have my full attention, I feel like a tween
Wow, the irony and what a magnificent plot
I'm on the edge of my seat, this really hit the spot
Closing credits, I guess it's time to exit
I'm better now and my life feels less hectic
It's amazing how a life can be reset to pristine
By enjoying the magic that takes place behind the screen

Humbleness in Motion

I'm a kind person, really, I am
I sincerely care for others, especially those considered Fam.
I don't brag or boast, it's just not my style
I prefer to remain low-key, my steelo is mild
Keep the attention because I don't need it
I prefer your trust and respect…you just can't beat it
Say hello to me and you will get it back
But it's cool if you prefer not, I'm not sidetracked
The Golden Rule…I believe in this motto
In my opinion, it's better than winning the lotto
I am what I am and cannot pretend
If one is not true to self, they cannot win
Taking kindness for weakness is a major fumble
Beware of the power that comes from remaining humble

Hustle

Monday through Friday, I punch the clock
On the weekends, I keep my home top notch
Work, work, work it never seems to end
Socially, I'm suffering and need to make amends
It's hard to break, I was raised like this
My dad instilled a work ethic and did not miss
Arise at 5 when I could barely talk
And work all day until I was too tired to walk
It's time for a change, this can't be right
It's time to say 'no' sometimes and build a life
I will also begin to remind myself often
Enjoy your life here before stretched out in a coffin
Hustle is important, I do agree
But moderation is vital to avoid insanity
I get it now and there will be change!
I'll take baby steps first so it's not so strange
There goes the alarm and I'm back on the grind
I'll change tomorrow, today there's no time

Smile Clown

If you're truly happy, prove it with a smile
Let's see those pearly whites for the pic, show everyone your style
Take a look at that friendly person; they're smiling ear to ear
I can let my guard down now, they have to be sincere
I'll trust them with everything, just look at those cheeks
With this person on my side losing is obsolete
I feel sorry for that dude mean-mugging, he must not be nice
I'd call the law on him with the quickness and wouldn't think twice
Oh no, there's trouble, let me find a friendly face
Looks like they're busy or cannot afford to catch a case
Well looka here, mean-mug is on his way
I wonder what he's going to fix his mouth to say
He didn't say a word and just came to help
I cannot believe my eyes, I'm ashamed of myself
Mean-mug saved the day and helped me out the jam
Then turned and said "if you need me brother, you know where I am"
I'll never judge him again for the size of his frown
Now it's understood why smiles are painted on clowns

Lucid Banality

This has to be a joke, where's the hidden cam?
Some people behave as if they don't give a damn
Tattoos and selfies, everyone's the same type
There's no honor in this, don't believe the hype
Live your own truths is what I always say
It appears nowadays, everyone has the same display
I wonder if the intent is to blend with the crowd
What happened to standing out, or is this not allowed?
Hop on the bandwagon, this makes it easy
Go with the flow, it's a lot less greasy
Until one day the voice from within
Makes it known just how this offends
Finally, as the light begins to shine
An attempt is made in the nick of time
"Hey, I'm a rebel and unlike anyone else!"
Settle down your man, take a look at yourself
You're 80 now and it's a little late
I respect your effort, but it doesn't change fate
What advice do you have now that the younger you couldn't see?
"Abstain from the ways of the world, don't end up like me"

Mea Culpa

To keep the peace, I must release
I need to face my reality to set my mind at ease
The journey gets wild in this crazy world
Strength is required or watch the world unfurl
I've made many mistakes as I reminisce
Consequences are accepted without complaints or hiss
Sometimes I'm not aware of an inadvertent infraction
But it's later revealed in an adverse action
If this is the case, my prayer is sent
Forgiveness is requested as I repent
Accountability is mandatory I do decree
For all my wrongs, I assume complete responsibility

Clean-Cut

Hey, what's up? How's it going?
That outfit is fly, and your skin is glowing
Very nice haircut and your beard is well-groomed
If you don't have a lady now, you're sure to get one soon
It's refreshing to see such immaculate appearance
It shows dignity and pride and self-care adherence
No sagging pants and no underwear in sight
A nice belt around your waist and your pants fit just right
That shirt is nice and compliments your frame
Those kicks are clean; I respect your shoe game
Keep it up young fella it's rare for your generation
You just may spark a change that impacts the whole nation
Note to the ladies in search of a real man
Find a clean-cut guy; your life will be grand

Note to Lil' len

Please to meet your acquaintance what a great opportunity
I have some information to share and it's strictly between you and me
You are very beautiful and so well loved
A blessing to many, thanks to the Man above
Establish your identity in whom He created you to be
Remember to love yourself first as you begin your journey
There will be highs and lows and all types of weather
Keep your head up and know your helper is keeping things together
Many disappointments will come from those you love most
Forgive them in spite of and spread love in extra dose
Make prayer and meditation a daily habit
Work hard to achieve your goals but respect the Sabbath
You were created to be great and do not settle for less
Put your plans in action and always give it your best
The things you desire most will come with obstacles and challenges
But the rewards will be great and much better than averages
You deserve the best and don't ever forget it
Always keep God first and your life will be lit
It seems like a lot but please take heed
This is the key to ensuring your destiny is achieved

Self-less

Forget the lime light & I don't want the attention
The superficial experience is too great to mention
God has blessed me, and I am very proud
But there's no need to send my pictures to the crowd
All is well today, and I have reasons to give thanks
But that single parent just found out there's no money in the bank
Is it all about me? Do I need to boast?
Surely there's more to life than reactions to a social media post
I think I will try my luck and stick with the Real
Because I don't need to solicit attention to validate how I feel
Thank God for life and the many, many blessings
But I am also sensitive to the needs of others and the things they may
 be stressing
Before the pictures of the new outfits and fancy meals
Consider your brother and sisters that may be struggling with an
 ordeal
In this life always remember this one true thing
The greatest experiences come from the joy loving others will bring

71/73

I felt you brother, thanks for sharing
It's one thing to know truth but to verbalize is caring
Blessed to see the real, I can definitely relate
Sometimes it feels like a curse, but we had to accept our fate
The gift is precious and not without purpose
Failure to act would have been a great disservice
The mission is tough but actually quite clever
Spark the brains that will create change for the better

Thanksgiving

I have a lot to be thankful for and give thanks daily
Anything less would be doing so frailly
I'm thankful for the good and the bad and the highs and lows
As I journey through this life, my appreciate only grows
I do respect the date set aside in November
Because it's marked on the calendar and helps us to remember
But I will give thanks until the end of time
Showing gratitude is free and doesn't cost a dime
So, I will continue my habit before each day is spent
Because thanksgiving isn't just a holiday but an everyday event

No

Nice to see you again, it's been a while
If I remember correctly, the last time my son was a child
I can appreciate your conditions and my heart goes out
I wouldn't wish that on anyone, that's a tough one- no doubt
No, I am not able to help you this time
I'm dealing with a few issues of my own
Your words are always kind and sweet, but your actions stand alone
I wish you the best and hope you're able to overcome
But please remove yourself from my presence this conversation is done

Final Score

No one knows the time or place
When the buzzer goes off calling an end to the race
I've lived my life as I felt it should be
I have no regrets. This has been an eventful journey
It was once stated that this place is not our home
This is my belief and is ingrained in my dome
So please don't feel sorry for me
God opened his door and I entered gladly
There should be no crying and behaving all wreck less
Be at peace and allow my spirit to rest
If I was able to make a difference in anyone's life
The honor goes to God and worshipping Him will suffice
Until we meet again, stay positive and true
Try to keep it real in everything you do
My body is gone from this place but remember this one thing
My love is still present behind the scene

Prayer

A moment of silence in this world of sin
Spilling my thoughts to no end
A question, a request, or simply giving thanks
From my heart to yours in a virtual clank
I need this commune for spiritual nourishment
Thank God for this blessing and option to vent
It doesn't take much in terms of minutes
Because what matters most happens in the spirit
At the end of each session, I'm redeemed and free
I'm ready to re-commit and live unselfishly
When I awake as my day begins
I plan to pray as much as possible; it's a sure win-win

Danger Zone

Go with the flow, I can see your point
Make everyone happy and do your best to anoint
Look, there's a transient, give him a wad of money
But put a little to the side for that fine young Honey
Give the extra offering because they really need it
Your well-being is important, just put it off a bit
The advertisement says to get it all at no expense
Live your life to the fullest, you can always repent
There's just one thing as you heed this advice
The consequences of such will not be nice
Enter if you wish but you're on your own
Because you will surely become a victim living in the danger zone

Adolesence

Young and carefree, oh what a time
Innocence ensured my world was divine
Growing up down south in the place called 'The Boot'
Very fond memories of the days in my youth
Santa was real to me like all other characters
They were my friends except the boogie man that scared us
Pretty girls made me smile and I wanted them all
I couldn't' wait to see bump into one hanging out at the mall
My bicycle was awesome; it got me from point A to B
I could go everywhere I wanted to, and the trip was free
Maybe I didn't appreciate it then because I wanted to be grown
The goal was to hurry up and leave the nest and make it on my own
There's no doubt that I should have cherished it more
My friends were plentiful then and good times galore
If I could turn back the hands of time, I would do so gladly
Because adulthood is just not all it was cracked up to be

Undercover Lover

With a warm beverage and cozy location
I love to unwind in private vacation
It doesn't cost a thing to live this dream
Just relax your mind and picture the theme
Page after page my curiosity is peaked
My imagination runs wild until the story is complete
What a wonderful way to escape the stress
Just grab a book and trust the process

Beastmode

Eternal peace is present, thanks to the gift from above
There isn't much that can be done to remove my love
When shots are fired, I often take the high road
But if a loved one is hurt, it's a different mode
God is in control and we possess His power
Sometimes I believe it becomes necessary to devour
When God gives permission to show evil whose boss
I vow to fight and avenge at all cost
Beast mode is activated and in full effect
This will remain until the enemy's in check
Mission complete and I'm chill again
Better think twice before harming family and friends

Oh...Word?

A man-made book no matter how long and clever
Will often fall short regardless of how it's put together
Words have different meanings based on the intended language
Interpreting context can leave translators in anguish
Human error also takes aim and threatens validity
It can alter the story far from the way it was intended to be
Whisper a message to a neighbor and pass it around
By the time it gets back to you, the truth cannot be found
One must also consider the elites and positions of power
Things are often changed to keep them from becoming sour
Sometimes things should not be taken verbatim
Proceed with caution and not on a whim
The good news is that there is a Helper within
Get to know Him before inquiring herein
Respect this guide and discover your truth
You'll then be prepared to tackle the uncouth

Hurlo

My first attempt in role as father
I was nervous at what the experience would offer
We bonded on Saturday nights while playing race car games
I tried to beat you, but outcome was always the same
It was my pleasure to escort you to and from school
Even when discipline was required for failing to follow the rules
But I also had your back when you were treated unfair
After I finished, all they could do was stare
From little league to doctor's appointment I aimed to please
It was my honor giving you the things you needed to succeed
You grew to be a man of many talents
I love the way you handle your business no matter the challenge
Blessed to be a part of your life and I will always treasure
My man Hurlo, I love you forever

Mirror, Mirror

Eyes closed as I imagine reflection
My reality is altered by pain and oppression
For years unable to break this cycle
Many attempts but all deemed trifle
Then one day I was forced to love another
Little did I know then what this act would uncover
Before I knew it, the curse was broken
No longer bound by such senseless notions
Now when I awake in the morning and need to see
Wow! God's creation as He intended it to be

Family Man

I don't need to go to the club to have a good time
Just give me love from family to unwind
Out every morning to provide for the family
But I can't wait to get back and escape the insanity
The calendar is marked for the next family vacation
Can't wait to relax and enjoy the libations
I love children's functions and try not to miss
Although they sometimes get embarrassed when I greet them with a kiss
I wouldn't trade my family for anything in the world
Their love is more precious than diamonds and pearls
Having lots of money is nice but could never compete
Because without my family, my life is incomplete

Visceral Consultation

Something doesn't seem right, what could it be?
Everyone else is doing it so it has to be me
But how can I ignore the voice from within?
I need to trust it to help keep me from sin
As I look around and contemplate
I noticed a correlation between actions and fate
Maybe it's not so bad to stand alone
I have to remember this place is not my home

Salad

Lettuce, tomatoes and bacon bits
By the time I'm finished this salad will be lit
Cucumbers, peppers, and even fresh spinach
I'll add the oil and vinegar after I'm finished
Ham, turkey, and a little shredded cheese
My stomach's growling and I aim to please
There you have it, favorite meal complete
Chat with you later, it's time to eat

Reunion

Come one, come all and gather around
No matter if you're near or out of town
Let's come together and enjoy godly fellowship
No agenda required, we'll shoot from the hip
The space will be filled with love and laughter
Even in disagreement we'll hug and make up after
We don't need a lot of money or fancy occasion
Just grab a t-shirt and enjoy the libations
The crawfish should be perfect come June
Much love family and hope to see everyone soon

Outlaw

Born with a spirit of unrest inside of me
Normal on the surface but true eyes can see
My parent saw it at an early age
And countered with work ethic before it reached the next stage
But yet and still the truth remains
You cannot deny the blood that runs through the veins
Rough, rugged and raw with a warm exterior
Sometimes I need to check the person staring back at me in the mirror
This is a world of sin and violence will not cease
But I make an extra effort to remain stable and live in peace

Reborn

Placed here without a choice
Out of my control because I had no voice
Bruised and misused like a punching bag
Then tossed to the side like an old used rag
This world hid what I needed to win
So, I flipped the script and tried it again
A true commune and relationship divine
I discovered truth in the nick of time
My Creator revealed the hypocrisy
It eradicated my past and set me free
Through prayer and meditation and remaining faithful
My world was never the same and I'm eternally grateful

Walking with Angels

TAMARA DEANNE HAWKINS

Unwavering

Father I am so very tired and weary.
Life has become so dark and dreary.

I feel my burden is such a heavy load.
I feel like I am failing if truth be told.

I cry to you to make me strong.
Please don't let these feelings last too long.

Help me make it through another day.
Help me bless others along the way.

You are my anchor through every stormy season.
I know my trials are for a good reason.

Forgive my doubt and the ways I have been behaving.
Through your undying love I will stand unwavering.

Hear My Plea

(from Jesus and me)

I definitely think I am losing my mind. I feel my sanity
slipping away a little more each day. What will I do
when it goes away? I live to be happy another day.
Well I don't know how long I have, but it doesn't seem long.
The question at hand is just how long do I have? It could
be hours; it could be days. It could be weeks; it could be
months. It could be years; it could be never. Who knows?
Is there anybody out there who can help me find the answers that
I seek? I hear a voice saying, "I can help you". I see before me a
common man. I think to myself how can he help me? From what
I see he is nothing special. I dismiss him because of his common
appearance. I go on a little farther and things are getting worse.
My trials seem too great, my burden too heavy. I feel
my soul crying out for help. Won't anybody help me?
Again, I hear a voice and it says, "Here I am". Once
again, this common man appears before my eyes.
How is it this common man thinks he can help me? I turn
away in disgust at this common man for I see no way for him
to help. Again, I begin my journey and find it even harder to
go on. I finally lose my footing and cry as I begin to fall.
In pain and anguish I see a hand reaching out. "Let me help
you", a voice says. It is the common man again. Reluctantly I
take his hand and to my surprise he lifts me up. He carries me
to his home and puts me in his bed and feeds me his food.
He stays with me until I am well and never leaves my side. I
ask him why and he answered as I cried "My name is Jesus.
I was sent here for you. All you had to do was trust me and
I would have helped sooner." As I looked into his eyes, I saw
a beauty I had never seen before. I was busy looking on the
outside to see what was on the inside. Now we travel together
in search for lost souls. Many who like me, who wait until they
fall. Sometimes there are those who never take his hand.

Just reach out, he is there for you. Take his hand and let him guide your path. That is all you have to do. Jesus gave his life so that we may live, and our hearts are all He asks us to give. Turn to him before it's to late. He is always there. I learned that despite his common appearance he is a very great man with unlimited strength and love. We all need to learn this simple lesson because it will save your life. I know I will be with Jesus forever and have eternal life. Will anyone join Jesus and me? Who will take his hand? Our journey leads to the promise land, everyone is welcome. My journey is so much easier now that there is someone here to help. If you need help just call his name. He won't be far. Come unto Jesus, he will give you rest. I hope to see you soon. An earnest plea from Jesus and me.

It's Time to Pray

The world is growing evil, it gets worse each day. On the
wind the Angels whisper "children it's time to pray."
A love one is ill they may die any day. Again, the Angels whisper,
"children it's time to pray."
When sorrow seems great and pain is here
to stay, gather up your strength for
it's time to pray.
When we lose our way and sometimes tend to stray,
we must fall to our knees for it's time to pray.
No matter what life holds or what struggles we face each
day, remember when they arise that it's time to pray.
God will be there for you to guide you on your way.
Don't forget each day that it's always time to pray.

Footprints in The Sky

This morning I looked up in the sky.
Staring at all the clouds with a sigh.
Then to my wonder, what do I see?
The footprints of God staring back at me.
The clouds had formed a pair of sandals.
I know that with God, there is nothing we can't handle.
I start each day with a simple prayer.
My love for God with others I share.
My foundation is grounded deep in the rock.
A am part of the good Shephard's flock.
Whenever trials come and my soul does cry,
I bring to mind the footprints in the sky.

Woman of Virtue

Hail thou woman of virtue.
To thy family you are true.
You show each day how much you care,
by taking all burdens to God in prayer.
You tend to all your family's needs,
while planting in them God's Holy seeds.
You teach them to walk on the Roman road.
They will never stray from what they've been told.
Fear not as your children grow,
The fruits of your labor will surely show.
Remember to pray each day, that God
will guide them along the way.
Hold your head high for God loves you.
Praises to you, woman of virtue.

My Prayer to You

I said a prayer for you today,
That God's hand would guide your way.
Through all your struggles and strife,
may God's mercy shine in your life.
May the Lord take you by the hand,
and lead you to a happier land.
Where everything is beautiful and bright,
with the brilliance of God's everlasting light.
When you are sad turn to David's Psalm,
and God will give you a gentle calm.
I pray that God will give you peace,
and that your sorrow will soon cease.
May God put love and joy in your heart,
So that from his way you will not depart.
My prayers are always with you,
That God will guide you through.

Thank You

My God you are truly worthy.
I give all that is in me.
I come to you with thanksgiving,
Praising that my God is living.
You are there for me every day.
Your loving hands guide my way.
Through all my turmoil and strife,
Your love is strong in my life.
You teach me of your loving truth,
The blessings I have are my living proof.
Thank you, God, for taking care of me.
Thank you for my place in Heaven for eternity.

Prayers During Trials

I think of the trials you are going through with a heavy sign.
My heart is burdened on your behalf, I feel like I could cry.
I pray each day for God to give you peace.
I pray the Holy Spirit will put your soul at ease.
I miss your friendship, your smile and laughter too.
I praise my Heavenly Father for all he has brought you through.
A trial by fire is truly not an easy one.
Praise be to God you are covered by the blood of the Holy Son.
One day soon you will be returning home.
By the grace of God from his will no more to roam.
Stay strong in his mercy my dear beloved friend.
He will sustain you until the very end.
Until you are free by grace from above, I wrote this
poem for you with all my Christian love.
Satan thinks he won when he accused you in God's sight.
Praise God he is wrong, for you are a child of light.
You are in my heart and in my prayers too.
You will come home a stronger man for all you have been through.
I can hardly wait for the day to see you face to face.
I know you are protected by God's unfailing grace.
God bless you and keep you until that day comes along.
We will rejoice and life praises to God with our song.

Prayer till Heaven

May the Lord shine blessings into your life.
May the Holy Spirit guide you through your strife.
Strength and peace fall from above,
Sent to you from the God of love.
As we walk through this life, held in God's hand,
We look ahead to the promised land.
I pray your soul is put at ease.
I pray your Faith in God does not cease.
Until the day we cross that sea,
Into Heaven for all eternity.

Prayer for Living in This World

Father God, please hold my hand.
Guide me through this foreign land;
Through fiery darts and dark mire.
Protect me from eternal fire.
Hold me in your loving arms.
Keep me safe from all harm.
Live in this world, but do not conform,
Until you take your heavenly form.
Grant me your unwavering peace.
Put my restless soul at ease.
Until the day of your return,
My soul for you alone will yearn.
Amen.

Broken Pieces

When my life began, it was a perfect plan. As I grew older, I wanted to do thing my way. I thought I knew what was best for me. I was the one living my life. I ran from your perfect plan. At first all was fine, and then I hit the bottom line. I lost my way and regretted the day that I thought I knew what was better for me. I have fallen so many times and have broken so many things. How can I be worthy of the love you gave to me?

I'm broken in pieces. How can I go on? Just look at what I have done to what you have given to me. I threw it away thinking it would be ok, if I left it for a while. How could I have known it would fall apart and become defiled? You trusted me and I let you down. I stand before you as a guilty child. I'm broken in pieces. Can you fix me, Daddy?

When your life began, I made a perfect plan. As you grew, you started pulling away. Even though I knew what was best, I put you to the test. I gave you free will for your life. You ran rom my perfect plan. You thought things were fine till you hit the bottom line. You lost your way and regretted the day you ran away from me. Though you have fallen many times and have broken your life. You will always be worth of the love that comes from me.

Just give me the pieces. I'll help you go on. I've seen all that you've done with what I gave. I held it for you when you walked away. You were gone for a while. It may have fallen apart and become defiled. Now you trust in me and I won't let you down. I stand before you as a loving father would.

Just give me the pieces and let them be fixed by me.

My life is brand new, I follow your plan. No more will I roam. My heart is yours to own. You know what is best. I made it through the test. I live for your perfect plan. Now everything is fine. I will reach the finish line. I've now found my way, no more regrets from that long-ago day. You fixed all the pieces.

Now I know I am worthy of the love you give to me.

No more broken pieces. Now I can go on. Now I will hold on to all you have given to me. Now all is ok. I will never walk away, not even for a while. The pieces are whole now, no long defiled. I trust in you and know you won't let me down. I stand before you a forgiven child. No more broken pieces. Thanks for fixing me, Daddy.

A Note to God and His Response

Oh, Father what a mess I've made of the life you gave me.
How can I look you in the eye?
What a disgrace you must see me.
Why can't I do what I know is right?

My child, do not despair, for my love is there.
Give me the pieces and I will fix it with care.
You will never be a disgrace to me.
I know what I have made you to be.
Trust me, my child, I will guide your way.
All I ask is that you obey.
All will be fine.
Everything is all right.
A am the one and only light.

Broken Heart

Father God my heart is broken and sore. I don't know if I can handle much more. Mourning for one as another one dies. My eyes are red from the tears I have cried. I ask for you to grant me peace, Father please put my soul at ease. I know they are both safe in your arms. Safe from all worldly harm. I pray for strength for all of my family. Let them know that they can lean on me. The one thing that helps us to cope, is the knowledge of God's eternal hope. We will se each other again one day. Then we will be together forever to stay. Thank you, God, for always being there. Thank you, God, for how much you care. Amen.

Rest in Me

My cry to God

I'm not here for me, I am only here for you. Without you here with
    me, there's nothing I can do.
I'm broken inside, I wish someone could see. I feel like I should hide,
    Father can you please fix me.
I wander through this life full of struggles and strife. I feel like I am
    blind, falling so far behind. I wish my path was clear so I can
    fully see. Father can you still the trembling fear in me.

God's response to me

Brokenness is a state of mind, regret is a waste of time.
Listen to the words I teach, forgiveness is within your reach.
Just listen to my still small voice, it's up to you. You have a choice.
I gave my son for you to be free, all I ask is you trust in me. Let go of
    the pain and leave it in the past. I will give you peace that will
    forever last.
I am always here for you, so find your rest in me.

What He Returns to You

We live in a world full of selfishness, always
wanting the best and expecting nothing less.
We live our lives full of fear, wondering if a true friend is near.
Our lives are filled with pain and despair, is
there anyone there who really cares.
Darkness comes and covers our sight,
hiding us from the one true light.
Anger, depression and bitterness reign,
leaving us with sorrow and pain.
When will we learn to let the past go, follow
the path that we should know?
How can we live a life of peace when we refuse
the one who can put us at ease?
The one who gave life back to the dead, the
one for our sins who suffered and bled.
He died for us and rose from the grave to each
who ask eternal life he gave. The peace God give
surpasses all, he lifts us up whenever we fall.
Why are we stubborn and stand our ground when
relief and comfort in Him are found?
The wickedness of our earthly flesh can he
transformed and be refreshed.
Let God take control of our life. He will end all pain and strife.
Our names are forever engraved in his hand, we will
be with him forever in the promised land.
Just trust in him and give Him your heart.
From our life he will never depart.
If you want the darkness forever to cease., just turn
to the only one who can give you peace.
Ask Jesus into your heart is all you need to do.
Peace, freedom, grace and love is what he returns to you.

A Sinner Becomes A Saint

Saints and sinners are not the same, for a
saint knows how to let go of shame.
A sinner holds on to their sin till they drop, their
pain and sorrow seems never to stop.
A saint is guided by God's tender hand, while
they travel through this foreign land.
A sinner is lost and wanders around, often
falling to the cold hard ground.
An amazing change can come about, when
a sinner lets go of all his doubt.
When a sinner surrenders to God without complaint,
that is when a sinner becomes a saint.

Storms of Life

Storms of life come and go.
Scars they leave God always knows.
The trials we bear will make us strong.
The trials will never last too long.
God doesn't give us a burden to bear without
sending Angels our load to share.
Angels come to us in many ways.
A stranger or friend we see each day. Some are given
small tasks to do, done unknown to me or you.
God see their deeds and knows their heart.
From his divine will they never part.
These Angels are gifts from Heaven above.
They are sent to us with abundant love.
I am thankful for Angels who are our friends.
Blessed to walk with them until the end.
Thank you for being the Angels you are.
We are the ones who have been blessed by far.
Thank you for sharing your heart full of love.
May God shower you with blessings from above.
May God always bless you and keep you.
Thank you for all the things you do.

Yes, Jesus is Enough

God gave us his only son to save us from our sin.
Faith and trust in Him are where we should begin.
God has chosen us to be his adopted heir.
The blessings of his son are what we all should share.
Some say it is enough he gave His only son.
He owes us nothing else when all is said and done.
My God tells me I should go to Him in prayer.
I should tell Him all my worries and all my cares.
A ask of Him my needs and all of my desires.
I trust Him as he leads me through my trials of fires.
My prayers may come as favors or out of desperation.
I earned the right to ask when I accepted my salvation.
God is my Father; a divine and Holy parent is He.
A simple child of God is all he asks me to be.
A parent never tells their child "I gave you life don't ask for
more". To turn their backs like that would cut them to the core.
My Father God has mercy and tells me every day. Pray to me and
I will hear every word you say, even though I ask Him favors when
things are getting tough. I can still proudly say Yes Jesus is Enough.

Control

I want control of my own life, I think I know what's best.
If you think I can't handle this, let's put it to a test.
I see it all in my mind the way things should be done, when
it all falls neatly into place, I'll know that I have won.
I will plan each little detail, and every little task.
When I pull it off alone, in my own glory I will bask.
I tried to do it all alone, and to my utter shame, when
everything fell apart, I alone was to blame.
Why did I think I could handle life all by myself?
Like a toy I had put God upon a shelf.
The pain, fear, and shame begin to grow inside of me.
I cried out to my Father as I dropped to my knees.
My God can you forgive me for this mess that I have made.
He answered to me gently, the price has already been paid.
God, I know the things I long for, the things I wish to do
will never come to past unless they come from you.
Now the torrential sea of my life becomes a gentle lull, Father
God I willingly submit myself and give you full control.

Fear of God

Faithfully father I will follow you. Guide
me through the trials of life.
Exhortations fall from my lips. I will share
your truth with the world.
Adoration fills my soul. You are my strength and my light.
Reverently I bow my head in prayer and bring you all my needs.

Obey your word and follow your will is the desire of my heart.
Freedom is what you have given me. The chains of death are gone.

Grace is poured from you down upon my
life. Grace, I do not deserve.
Observe your law and guidance. You always know what's best.
Debt free is what I am. You paid the price in full.

I live my life the only way I know with a true and
holy Fear of God to the world I daily show.

Worthy

I have made mistakes in my life.
I have gone through struggles and strife.
I have failed so many tests.
I have not always done my best.
I am full of doubt and worry.
I feel that I am not worthy.
God has been there from day one.
God sent us his only son.
God sees me through struggles and strife.
God is the guide of my life.
God tells me there is no reason to worry.
God reassures me I am always worthy.

In Plain Sight

I will not shed another tear.
I guard my feelings out of fear.
I build a wall around my heart, so it won't be torn apart.
My true feelings I will not tell.
I will only say that all is well.
Weary, worn and so very tattered, my heart is done being shattered.
To God alone can make the repairs.
If you really believe that all is all right, you
missed the truth hiding in plain sight.

T'was the night before Thanksgiving and what do I spy?
The most perfectly delicious looking chocolate pie.
The temptation was great to say the least,
so, each of us had one perfect piece.
We ate the pie early but do not despair,
tomorrow the rest of the pie will still be there.

Happy Thanksgiving!

Whisper My Angel and I Will Follow

BETTY WINKLER

Who Am I?

In my memory I can't recall
Ever being bad at all.
The picture of me that's in my mind?
Is a loving person, warm and kind?
But deep inside, perhaps secretly;
I often wonder what others see.
If I saw the picture of me, they paint
Would I see a devil, or a saint!
Not knowing which, I'll go on walking tall
Maybe thinking I'm someone I'm not at all.

Betty Winkler

Which Face?

Which face will I wear tonight?
I think I'll wear my face that's bright.
I'll put it on before I go
The face I want my friends to know,
And which face will I show to you?
If we should meet, as we might do?
I think I'll wear my face that's glad,
And keep my real face hid that's sad.
There are many faces I must wear
Because my true face shows despair,
My faces are a good disguise, unless you look into my eyes
And then you'll see my heartbreak there,
Which face will I wear?

Betty Winkler

I am not allowed to run the train
The whistle I can't blow
I am not allowed to say how far the RR cars can go
I am not allowed to blow off steam
Nor even clang the bell
But let it jump the GD track
And see who catches hell

No wonder we don't communicate
You say you understand what I said
But what you don't know is that what you heard
Is not what I meant.

Betty Winkler

My wallet is thinner, my feet are sore;
From shopping and tromping around each store
The candy is made, the cookies are baking
My goodness no wonder my back is aching!
While working I'm thinking… it would be grand
If I knew where to purchase just one more hand.
Thoughts come to mind that bring me cheer
As I prepare for Old St. Nick this year
And though time and miles keep us apart,
I keep my loved ones in my heart
So, by gosh – by golly – by Xmas morn,
If I survive – broke – tired – and worn,
I'll be wishing you happiness, health, and cheer,
And prosperity through the coming year.

Betty Winkler

One Picture

I nearly got hooked again.
Trapped by memories of what has been.
Trapped by knowing that you're still there
And by rumors that you still care.
I nearly got hooked again.

Forgetting that one and one make two,
I nearly went back to loving you.
But I took my scrapbook out to see
A photo that was given me,
And seeing her there by your side
The old love blooming quickly died.
But I nearly got hooked again.

Amen, Amen, Amen.

Betty Winkler

My Angel

You were an angel when you were two
And I did what e'er you'd bid me do.
If I left the house when you were about
I first would have to take you out
For you'd stand in the door and cry for me
And tears aren't for angels, so naturally
I'd pick you up- and off we'd go -
Me and my angel of long ago.
Fate was unkind and for many years
I was not there to halt your tears.
I did not get to watch you grow -
My little angel of long ago.
Now I have found you, you are grown
With two angels all your own.
And this time fate has smiled on me
She took one angel – but brought me three.

Betty Winkler

Kin

I scan the picture carefully, I scrutinize the face,
Is there some resemblance to me? No, I see not a trace.
My sister's child how could that be? It was said
  my sister looked like me.
I puzzle silently and read the letter, and I smile,
Two gifted nephews, why of course, I knew that
  all the while,
Her beauty comes from her dad's side of the family,
But two gifted nephews, now I boast
Their brains they got from me!

Betty Winkler

Hard Times!!!

The car's in the shop, there's a dental bill,
But I keep saying I'll save, and I will!
Last week the central air went out
When I paid the bill, I had to shout.
Financially this struggle is killing me
This week by week emergency.
A month ago, I had the plumber in,
Now it looks like he'll have to come again.
To get ahead now sure takes skill
But I keep saying I'll save, and I will!
It may take a hundred years or so
To learn everything that I must know
Mechanics, plumbing, dentistry,
Air conditioning and some carpentry.
After paying for learning every skill,
If I live long enough, I'll save…. I will!

Betty Winkler

Gus

When I come home each night and sometimes the world's not right,
Who's always there to cheer me up?
My dog.
Who always listens when I talk, who's always ready for a walk?
My dog.
Who would never ever leave me, who would never think to grieve me?
No one else…my dog.
And who am I just wild about, someone I can't do without,
Yep you're right,…Old Gus.

Betty Winkler

I searched for Knights in Shining Armor
  in every store and mall
I looked for words of wisdom to hang upon your wall.
I priced some gifts of solid gold
  and some that were real thrillers
But alas I'm sad to say my box
  is full of stocking fillers.

Oh, thank Heavens
for 7-11!!

Betty Winkler

Merry Christmas to you and yours -
    because yours belongs to me
That is why there will be no tags -
    around my Christmas tree.

I have sinned and I've been punished,
    now to God I pray
Please don't let them take my child,
    my very life away.
So, if I get her back again,
    please try not to be sad
Because you are this someone who
    I have always had
But if fate should be unkind -
    and she is yours to keep
Make all of her Christmases happy,
    because in my heart I'll weep.
So Merry Christmas to you and yours -
    because yours belongs to me
That is why there will be no tags
around my Christmas tree.

Betty Winkler

With the special strength you possess,
You drove away my fears and stress
When I was blind,
T'was you who helped me see.

Betty Winkler

To Lulu With Love

I wake, and for an instant reality's untrue,
The cold reality that we will soon be losing you.
Our efforts to hold onto you have only been in vain
To hold you any longer now would only cause you pain.

With trusting heart you've given us all that you could give,
And we shall love you dearly as long as we shall live.
Now the time has come dear heart when we must set you free
Though you will live within our hearts for all eternity.

Betty Winkler

Our Old Neighborhood

I went back to visit our neighborhood
My visit brought memories, like I knew it would.
But, just for a moment, the past seemed untrue,
And I was there once again on my way to meet you.
I went back to visit our old neighborhood
They're building a bank where the Hickory House stood.
The streets are too quiet now, the laughter is gone,
Our friends that we knew there, like us, have moved on.
I went back to see where we lived once again,
Though the house is still standing, I didn't go in
I knew that the memories, just waiting inside
Would quickly bring tears I was trying to hide
Yes, I went back to visit our old neighborhood
The visit brought memories, like I knew it would
The memories brought heartaches, and sadness anew
For I knew I was searching in vain there for you.

Betty Winkler

My Heart Got in My Way

I'd like to know who wrote that song
That came right from my heart
I just heard all the words, I've tried to say
I've tried to say them many times,
But every time I'd start
This silly heart of mine got in my way.

Now those words right from my heart
Are number one on every chart
And when you hear them, I'm sure you'll agree
Someone wrote a song for you and me.

I'd like to know who wrote that song
Someone else has come along
And written every word I've tried to say
About these feelings deep inside
Oh, how many times I've tried to say them
But my heart got in my way.

Betty Winkler

Life

Read these poems and you will see
My thoughts of things that used to be.
The happy times were far and few
So, these I have not shown to you.
There's been some laughter, and some strife,
The same that's found in every life,
Still I'll leave this life with no regret
For there's nothing that can beat it yet!

That's life.

Betty Winkler

A Prayer

Lord, keep me from the habit of thinking
I must say something on every subject and on
every occasion.
　　Release me from the craving to straighten
out everybody's affairs.
　　Keep my mind free from the recital of endless details --
give me wings to get to the point.
　　I ask for grace enough to listen to the tales
of others' pains. Help me to endure them with patience.
　　But seal my lips on my own aches and pains,
they are increasing and my love of rehearsing them
is becoming sweeter as the years go by.
　　Teach me the glorious lesson that occasionally
it is possible that I may be mistaken.
　　Keep me reasonably sweet; I do not want to be a saint --
some of them are so hard to live with --
but a sour old person is one of the crowning works
of the devil.
　　Give me the ability to see good things in
unexpected people. And give me, O Lord, the grace
to tell them so.
　　Make me thoughtful, but not moody; helpful,
but not bossy. With my vast store of wisdom, it seems
a pity not to use it at all -- but Thou knowest, Lord,
that I want a few friends at the end.

Betty Winkler

Written for Ruth

The tie that binds us is you and I
    As sister and as brother
Is a gift of birth as we entered earth
    That was given by our mother
She gave a special gift to you
An inner strength that all delight to see
And the tie that binds us, you and I
    was her special gift to me.
We traveled many hard roads as we've
    wandered thru the years
We shared each other's laughter and we
    shared many tears
And many, many times before
When despair has knocked upon my door
T'was then the golden tie brought
    you to me
With that special strength that you possess
    You drove away my fears and stress
When I was blind t'was you taught
    me to see
Now it's hard for me to say
    what I feel in my heart today
I surely hesitate to even try
I'm proud of who and what you are
And admit it seems a bit bizarre
    for whoever would have thought that I
Who received this special gift of birth?
The most special gift on earth
The tie that binds us to each other
Would someday have the right to say
    and oh, how I delight to say
That preacher over there is my kid brother!

Betty Winkler

What I can give is never as much
    as I get from giving.

Betty Winkler

2)   To withdraw from an argument
    does not make you the winner,
    but what you have saved
    is your own dignity and grace.

Betty Winkler

If you think you are beaten, you are,
If you think you dare not, you don't;
If you like to win, but think you can't
It's almost a cinch you won't
If you think you'll lose, you've lost,
For out in the world you find
Success begins with a fellow's will;
It's all in the state of mind.
Full many a race is lost
Ere ever a step is run;
And many a coward fails
Ere ever his work's begun.
Think big and your deeds will grow,
Think small and you'll fall behind,
Think that you can, and you will;
It's all in the state of the mind.
If you think you're outclassed, you are;
You've got to think high to rise;
You've got to be sure of yourself before
You can ever win a prize,
Life's battles don't always go
To the stronger or faster man,
But sooner or later the man who wins
Is the fellow who thinks he can.

Betty Winkler

Merry Christmas

After the wrapping from each package is torn
We thought you might be frazzled this Christmas morn.
So, we searched for the perfect way to make
The two of you take a restful break.
So, we're sending along some good hot brew
And old Willie to sing some songs for you.
And a Christmas toast from me,
May your cup runneth over in '83!

Betty Winkler

The Lyrical Point of View

This is dedicated to my people who are mentally diagnosed and to Ms. Yvette Bell, the wonderful woman who taught me that I am enough.

MUSA LANG

"The Musician or The Note"

There once was a musician- who saw through a scope
The lovely pair of eyes on a musical note
He never heard one that carried such beauty
So, getting to know her became his main duty
"Who are you?" he asked. "Where are you from?"
And then her reply was "From the light of the Sun.
I saw through my optics your style had a bling
In the words of my Goddess, 'You were doing your thing'.
The Note told the Musician, "We need to team up
I've watched you through the years- your style has cleaned up
We met not by accident- in this…please trust
Your soul is purer than all humans from dust
Other men wouldn't care as much as you do
Or take interest in musical love…it's true
Take it from me…a note that's unheard
By any other living human being that's my word
Mankind- so selfish- undeserving of sound
You sharpen your swords- and put one another down
My Goddess Decibella- is mighty not little
And will bless you greatly- if you solve her riddle
'Which came first: The Musician or the Note?'"
The Musician grew silent and paused for a while
And after a few moments his cheeks bore a smile
Finally, he said "They both express love
And want to be remembered through pain and through hugs
They both need each other-every chime with every rhyme
They therefore came together-every beat-every time
So, the Note said: "Despite any ill-living-and any man's wrongs
Decibella's gift is my use in your songs
Teach my character to your fellow man
Spread truth of my existence all through the land
I'll contact some cousins, you call up your band
And we'll have the best jam session ever to jam

"Roses"

The meaning always underlying
These flowers never closed
To the open soul and giving heart
That shows up with a rose
Inside a glance one takes a chance
At finding visual bliss
And with the luck that falls as dice
One also finds a kiss
If love is felt a rose can surely
Speak from such a stance
And guys should hide one at their back
And then ask for a dance
Since life is short and sometimes opportunities
Are not born
Confess your feelings- share a rose...
But beware of its thorn

"Prayer"

When the time comes to communicate
With the Creator up above
We meditate to listen
And use prayer to speak with love
That Higher Power listens to your heart
Not just your lips
And having prayer to respect and share
Is truly a thoughtful gift
The Lord's open-door policy
Never falters nor does it slip
He's never too busy to hear you out
He's available all three shifts
Just follow the light that leads your soul
The glow is brilliant white
It guides the way to eternal bliss
And shows you wrong from right

"Teddy Bear"

It'll never squeal and never leak
The secrets that you share
So, feel free to go confide
Them with your Teddy Bear
The scruffy touch is never rough
So, hug em' all you wish
It's within reach -so enjoy the plush
Sensation as a gift
No matter how grim or gruesome
The news you give- they always smile
Or maintain their poker face
To coax the innocent child
Anyone healed from a broken heart
Knows exactly what it means
To the person ill who happens to have
A Teddy Bear on their team

"Bed"

After a tiresome day- I'm glad to lay
And rest my sleepy head
And then awaken- still not shaken
In the comforts of my bed
When I remove my sandals- I climb upon it
Anticipating sweet dreams
As soon as I brush my teeth
And wash my face until it's clean
Next, I snuggle underneath
The covers- to feel snug
Then stretch outright or get in the fetal
And give myself a hug
In hindsight I think on times
I've slept like a rock or lead
I always find I should give thanks
That I can enjoy my bed

"The Color of Character"

We are all imperfect- Dear Lord, please forgive us for our sins
And remind us that good character's worth more than color of skin
Demonstrating with nonviolence -some thought it was foolish and weak
But one day I read and heard of it said a key that set me free
Dr. Martin Luther King Jr. fought for my rights when we needed change
Simply because his integrity outweighed his discomfort and pain
All human beings can have hope- and the peace they've never known
By seeing that we are all one spirit- the truth that's hardly shown
My predecessors broke segregation in the name of brotherly love
For our opportunity to live free and help one another trudge
Now my black friends and white friends can socialize as they please
So, we pray together and decay whenever our time is called to leave

"Butterflies in the Garden"

The reds and greens and shades of grey
Are easy to display
By butterflies
Which share the magic of color a special way
When they catch the eyes- they magnify
Mother Nature's hidden secrets
Her strengths are sometimes softly shown
But are not to be viewed as weakness
Whether orange or black- the colors match
The mood of the presence of beauty
From pink to blue they do pursue
A lifestyle where elegance is duty
So, question the sparkle of a garden
Where herbs and veggies do blossom
And hopefully- you too will see
A butterfly's presence is awesome

"Love Doctor"

If love was my patient, could I keep its heart beating?
Could I take away the aches and pains caused by hurt and cheating?
Could I heal it up and patch it up- and give a new beginning?
To the one thing of which whose death would amount to the total
    ending
If love were my patient- would I have the courage
To find and punish the one who struck her down and attempted her
    murder
Oh, how could I be- he- to inject the needle of adrenaline to the heart
And not weep for coming so close to the end of a wonderful start
If love were my patient- how could I be brave
To rush into that emergency room- knowing I had to save
The one who gave us sunlight and air- all luxuries
That I trampled on and took for granted, especially breath to breathe?
How will my surgical efforts turn out? I really do not know
Was I precise with Him under the knife- did I focus high and low?
If I sit here stressing- it will not help- my mental gasket will blow
I guess all I can do is love myself- and time will surely show

"The Warden of My Craft"

My creativity's doing time…locked behind a glass
The watch bezel is what I call the warden of my craft
I push- I fight- I struggle hard to give my poem feast
For I have fans with antsy hands- that hunger like a beast
With every stroke this pen makes- I feel their souls quiver
Cause' once anxiety settles in- I feel I must deliver
At poem number forty-five, I thought my work was finished
Until a fan had read them all- and asked for more, for instance
I dropped my head and felt as though I'd nothing left to give
Then asked myself, "Is this the life a poet has to live?"
The inspirations long-gone, or far beyond my span
Then next I had an epiphany that led me to a plan
So, listen close and hear me well until you understand
How poem number forty-six stumbled upon this man
I went without a writing tool for days that turned to weeks
And waited oh so patiently for inspiration to speak
And right before I deemed it all no more than foolish hope
I lifted my pad from the trash- for inspiration spoke
The voice said "Respect time, it tempers…so don't force it
The quality that it creates makes a masterpiece gorgeous
To make this story short…forty-six made it to print
And since I learned to be inspired- it rose beyond the lint
An hourglass can do no harm, and this to you I'll pass
My personal impatience is what locked away my craft

"Ice Cream"

What's your favorite ice cream?
Mine is peanut butter and fudge
I can't be saved from when I crave
A chunky cone to indulge
It's sweet, smooth delectable, tasty with each swallow
So scrumptious- you could lose your head like the Legend of Sleepy
    Hollow
I've eaten it all- I can't recall the flavor I last ate
You can enjoy it solo on your own or share it with your mate
If you eat too fast- you just might have
A jolt of brain freeze
Just take it slight- and slow your bites
So that the frost will ease

"Colors"

What do colors mean to me?
Do they symbolize success?
Do they speak to guys who rest their eyes?
On pants with matching vests?
What do colors mean to me?
Encouragement from the start
To see the nation's flag fly
While troops commence to march
What do colors mean to me?
A camouflage for eyes
For chameleons or a cocoon
That brings a butterfly
What do colors mean to me?
An artist with her pad
Who earns her cents and pays her rent?
Depending on her craft
Life is full of so much beauty
To enjoy, embrace, and share
So please feel free to come partake
In its variety of dares-
Dare to shine Dare to sparkle
Dare to show your colors bright
You're wonderful… so let your glow illuminate the night

"Abyss"

If a heart is not pure, does it really exist?
The answer to this riddle can only be found in the abyss
When a shark consumes a minnow, is the act cruel and hateful?
Or does this creature bask in its appetite for the tasteful?
When a leg of lamb or steak kabob is served, I tend to grub
In the same way this so-called "monster" shows its tummy love
I want to be a friend of me- and not the person I used to be
What is the cost? What is the loss- please minimize the fee?
Can that which is deep lose depth if truth is ever shallow?
The steady embrace of it all is that which should be hallowed
Am I just a man with a jester's plan for seeking purity?
Or have I set foot on a path to discover the good in you and me
The Universe is mental- for wiser men have spoken
For admission into the mental abyss- these words could be the token
So, one thinks- so they become in time or in that moment
The overflow of all your want's within- as soon as you own it
The mind is like a vast sea with never ending borders
It's all coming…whatever you summon- the bait is simply your order
At your command, by your demand- is your possession I'm sure
And yours to keep- no lies, no cheat- if what you seek is pure
The abyss I believe- is in need of a search from time to time
But I know that keeping love inside my heart will help me thrive
My soul is alive- breathing, living, smiling deep within
On difficult days by giving praise- gratitude comes again
A poet I am- and one I'll remain- a lowly position upon the chain
But I searched the abyss and discovered love that satisfies me to the rim
I thank you for taking this journey with me to solve a case you needed
    to close
The journey was long- but we survived, so here's the question I wish
    to pose
If a person's heart contains no love, does it really exist?
You no longer need me as your guide- the answer lies in your abyss

"Mistakes"

The mistakes I make can't break me
But they can make me
When I look at the world around me, I see souls feeling their way
    through life
Hoping to find the path to lead them to what they know deep down
    within will quench the thirst
Which is created by failures
My failures are props used by a magician: now you see a difficulty,
    now you don't.
I know now that what I see, even in its very essence is
Merely what I wish. Seek and ye shall find has been written before.
If the sun hides behind the clouds, what I see tends to be negative.
If the sun has shown favor upon me and shines bright through and
    through the
Darkest places in my mind, it is registered as a positive morning.
Is it a mistake to experience a rough day?
Only the wisest of fellows and most experienced of ladies, perhaps,
    would know.
I'm quite unsure myself…being only a lowly poet. However,
I do believe that the mistakes I make can't break me,
But they can make me stronger.

"Wind"

The wind is such a hard worker- it deserves a better pay!
More than complements and good things we humans write and say
Like…" Gosh, the weather's wonderful," and "It's such a beautiful day."
She even carries the kites in the sky so the children below can play
But what's behind this awesome force- is it magic? Science? Inertia?
It's always on like Saturday morning cartoons- without commercials
Now I know just a little- but humor this riddle- without wind, where
    would we be?
I hope that I never will need to find out, since wind is so kind to me

"Journey to the King"

I traveled to see the king
To request food for my family
Famine struck my land
But it's just the card God handed me
My kin were oh so loving, even though we were so poor
And evil's so seductive it just wants us to seek more
Along the lengthy trip, I was stopped by a lion
Who told me if I followed him, he'd finalize my crying?
I simply just ignored him, and I said "I need the king"
My family needs some food to eat- the most important thing
I also found a golden lamp that's worth a billion shekels
And heard a twisted voice highlight a choice that seemed to heckle
My conscience- it however thundered loud enough to burn me
I stalled not a step, but focused harder on my journey
And next I was tempted by a harlot near some trees
Who promised she had everything I'd ever want and need?
She was alluring and seemed assuring as though she'd meet my wishes
Despite its all- I turned her down- to proceed with my mission
I finally arrived at the palace- calling at its' gates
The bridge was lowered- I crossed the moat- there was no time to waste
Desperate for the king's grain, I eagerly told a guard
That my family was indigent and that my throat was parched
He handed me a goblet of water to replenish
Put it aside and fetched the king as soon as I was finished
The king approached and as I bowed, I couldn't help but notice
The satchels full of grain and golden lamps that met my focus
The king told me because of my resistance to temptation
I truly did possess the heart to wisely rule a nation
He blessed me with great wealth and golden lamps galore
I gave God His praise as my face hit the floor
And just when I thought the king's blessings had come to an end
He told me he had something special he wanted to throw in
He hinted it was for my wife and tailored just for her
This is no joke. It was a coat of female lion's fur.

"My Buddy's Lost Wing"

I once saw a fairy- missing her wing
Helping her find it would be the right thing
We lifted a mountain and unearthed some soil
And tracked through some geysers til' our feet started to boil
But then I woke up and it was only a dream
And for a while I hoped I could return to that scene
Oh, how I longed for that fairy's company again
For we had so much fun
I began to wish I lived solely in her realm instead of reality
I saw the Great star and wished upon it so
One day, I bumped into a fairy who looked down and out
I asked her what her trouble was.
She said she had a friend who misplaced his wallet and
That she was having difficulty finding it for him.
So, I assisted in the search that took us to the far regions of the earth.
Somewhere near a Scandinavian village, she discovered it
And picked it up and said, "Thanks for helping me look for my
chum's wallet."
She handed the wallet to me. I didn't realize that the wallet resembled
mine
So closely until she said she would see me again soon. And just as
certain
As the bees carry pollen, the wallet was my own. My friend
disappeared.
I once saw a fairy missing her wing and I'm glad I had a conscience
to do the right thing.

"Broken Wing"

I feel as though chickens have a legitimate excuse for not flying. You see,
They weren't meant to fly, they were meant to fry.
What excuse have I?
Peer pressure, none the lesser, prevents he who can move mountains
     with his faith
And cause the kingdom of his to quake, to crumble, quiver and break
And all this depends upon the quality of the company of which he
     associates
How can such a man or woman thrive and survive long enough to
     have a testimony
As to how he or she managed to stay alive?
I believe a chap of this nature must have the motivation and drive
     that's generated
Not externally, but from his or her inside.
You see, my sisters and brothers:
We were all put here to learn to spark the wind beneath one another
And inspire upper exploration…
To teach each other to soar the atmosphere
Without doubt or fear…to motivate those
Trapped within their delusions to make an honest reality their
     conclusion.
You see, I know that the mistakes I've made have created a present
That consists of enduring the pain of my broken wing…
But I'm still focused on flying up high in the sky
Because that just happens to be the right thing
And the discomfort, I'll take it
With resilience, I'll make it
We all stumble…it's true. I won't fake it.
After all, this broken wing will heal in time with self-care,
And with a good bit of patience

"More"

Can I be…more than the grains of sand on the coastal shore?
Is it too much to ask that I be more than a simple shadow cast?
In a dim location where existence is so vast? I beg of my fellows
To vouch with a bellow great praise on my behalf
That doesn't distain but conquers and lasts.
Sometimes I feel I don't deserve much.
But of a twinkle of a smile, I sense I'm owed a touch
Can I be…one of the happiest souls in the pool of awesome people
Who make this world a better place?
By just being willing to be free of fear
And lend an honest ear
To help anyone who needs it, provided they are near
Humanity is a gift from above, such as love
Through any turmoil every person is worthy of a hug.
I pray I am not asking too much by wishing all to have
The feel and look that is so smug
Can I have more?
For instance, a shred of hope that lies in the distance
It consists of more than a simple existence,
But doesn't have to be long-listed.
If my desire isn't ill-shifted
May I continue witnessing the blessings of the gifted,
And
At least continue to inspire others and aspire to
Please, perhaps be…more?

"The Necessity of Leisure"

I fish with the best. My rod you can test
Relaxing…the search for bass
Some actions I take- it's true, not fake-
For fun- not for sake of cash
You ponder- I riddle- we punt, and we dribble
It's overtime once and again
I practice un-hired, until I'm too tired
While others take comfort in gin
Another man's hobby may be his folly
Take care as you tend to your sports
Know safety's importance as chief amongst options-
Be not simple minded…of course
So, look and you'll find a way to unwind
And let all the stress fall aside
It's just like a boulder- too much for your shoulders
To give it a permanent ride
So, go on vacation- or travel- or cruise
Spend some time without waking up groggy
If it's reading the news- or hearing some blues
Always make time for your hobby

"Running Low on Fuel"

I'm running low on fuel today- but striving to be a winner
But can't survive and stay alive without breakfast, lunch and dinner
I got a good bit of exercise drank some cups of water
And now I'm feeling burned out for not listening to my father
He told me to eat vegetables and don't forget to rest
Or else this mind will wander off- even though I try my best
Tomorrow is a new day- for me to turn it around
Just look at me- and you will see- that for success I'm bound
I'm running low on fuel today- or maybe it's just the sensor
My oil is bad- and now my ride is on a gasoline binder
It's a nice car with a warranty- I'd be a fool to chuck it
But an oil change is pertinent, if I want to save some ducats
However, on the brighter side- my engine isn't shot
It'll only take about twenty minutes if I take it to the shop
Tomorrow is a new day for me to turn it around
Just look at me- and you will see- that for success I'm bound
I'm running low on fuel today- I learned that I'm a sinner
I know that in my prayer life, I'm still just a beginner
No one's perfect but the LORD- who's always in control
So, I'm leaving earth one day at a time- as death will take its tole
I'll ask the LORD for motivation- cause' that's the fuel I need
He's awesome- though I do not ask, He gives me air to breath
Tomorrow is a new day for me to turn it around
Just look at me- and you will see- that for success I'm bound

"Our Shine"

There's a star in the sky
On behalf of You and I
Reflecting the glow within us
Even from the shy
If the heartless dwells in darkness
The moon begins to brighten
When the scales that watch your shoulders' weight
Tilt and start to lighten
Delighted when the stresses
Are remove- one will find it…
Really easy to be full of joy
To share and will not hide it
From a metaphor- love better pour
And leave a trail behind
Just like a cosmic radiance
We all deserve to shine

"Poetry and Love"

My soul feels captured- a prisoner behind bars
Encapsulated by barbs that leave such painful scars
It bangs on the walls that make him feel trapped
Until he sheds something that's more than just a rap
My soul feels captured- did you hear the verbs
That flow from that woman with rich spoken words?
It seems presidential…the way the notes hit
Prepared to rule nations they seem to have fit
My soul feels captured- please feel my fire
As I talk about my life and these chains of desire
Like a beast in a cage with a mic without lager
This globe is so full of folks needing my swagger
Please feel my soul- it's rough- and it's cuffed
I started as a rapper now poetry's enough
If you can't taste my love- then inhale my musk
As I die in love with life and turn back to dust

"How Much Love?"

How much does it love me?
It rises in the east and sets in the west
It doesn't take sick days or complain about stress
When compared to extremes it passes all tests
And it's always in rotation-never stops to rest
How much does she love me?
The snow- it fell so quick
But she's up early ironing to dress me up thick
And drives me to school- education is a gift
Mom even packed my lunch- and did it so swift
How much does he love me?
He works so hard on the job
And even on the weekends he's out laboring in the yard
Taking care of my family the very best he can
And he emphasized the value of being a good man
How much do I love me?
I know I have faults
But I suture the wounds I cause myself and try not to add any salt
And I don't mind helping others- my pride tossed away to the left
Because respecting my brethren is a form of loving myself
How much does He love us?
You know…what's His name?
The One who blessed me by making sure His beloved son came
Some call Him 'King of Kings' as His shine is the 'Bling of Blings'
How often do we love all the wrong things?

"The Love She Has for Me"

In a sense, it's quite unexplainable, yet to my surprise
The Love was obtainable. This love she has for me is beyond weight
and measure.
She haphazardly pleases me, and she mimics the same pleasure.
This "Love" thing is unusual, for I have never before lived through
Anything so enriched with natural feel-good. When I am going
through mood-swings that sway
As though they are mocking the motion of a pendulum, I can't help
but feel she is pushing the swing;
Much like a parent pushes a child's playground instrument. When
it's over, she quotes the words of
Comical treasure spoken by comedians of old as we fill our bellies
with giggles and feel our souls dash
Through time without gravity while our tongues quiver with laugh-
ter. When I am ill, I am halted
In my footsteps as she demands that my fully-planned day's itinerary
be replaced
With bedrest as she medicates my feeble body.
She monitors my temperature and applies cold compresses to my
forehead;
Eagerly standing watch moment by moment, as if my healing will be
instantaneous and
Surprising, like when the suspense has ended after winding a
jack-in-the-box.
The Love we have uses no compass, carries no whips to enforce
change, neither denies
Or neglects; it doesn't rewind itself and doesn't promote fast forward-
ing. Our Love somehow
Rests and dwells in a stationary position of ultimate bliss at its peak.
It feels like money in my pockets that attract everything worth hav-
ing without
My having to take out a loan.
Unexplainable what happens to be: A strange thing The Love She
Has for Me

"Sweet Experiences"

Do you recognize the quality of splendor within bliss?
For therein lies the wonder that a sweet experience gives.
Ever ponder what the next lad will say and feel
Or how deeply they may smile after spending some time
Playing with a puppy? The wheels of their imagination shall
Spin and turn and twirl. At the same time, a baby doll
Will be given as a gift to a small girl. One can find
The same elation expressed on the faces of little ones
As the ice cream parlor doors swing open by the force and
Energy of their own hands. Even a curious scientist finds
A moment of greatness as they study a petri dish and
Discover a hidden truth that may heal another. Is rain
Simply rain, or is it a divine children's toy that provides
A small puddle for a young one to leap into: For is that not
A special, perfect, and sweet experience? Sure, a queen's ice cream
Cone is a key component of her sweet experience, but does
The experience limits its reach to her alone? Or do the ants
That may crawl and march beneath her feet partake
In the festivities at the site of the melted drop
Once it rolls from the cone and reaches the ground? Perhaps
It would be wise for me to conclude that life's sweet experiences
Are sometimes meant to be shared, and not spared

"Unconditional Love"

Now I'm not sure we see eye to eye
That beauty and truth that cannot lie
Which is called Unconditional Love
Like waters of life, it's ever flowing
Or like an evergreen tree- it's constantly growing
When I speak of it all- my soul begins glowing
And wish to hug myself- without consciously knowing
If it's winter in your heart and you can't stop the snowing
Please have faith in this moment- it's splendid- don't blow it
I dabble and dibble with words all the time
But don't you dare miss the value I place in this rhyme...
For it speaks of Unconditional Love
Like, when mom issued spankings when I acted a heathen
And later dad mimicked, though I was previously beaten
And sent to my room without my dinner that evening
And left with no television to ponder the reason
Why? It was Unconditional Love
Mountains sit high- from valley to crest
I love myself better- but the Lord loves me best
If He didn't- why would He give life, then rest?
I'm sure I know the power of the breath in my chest...
It's Unconditional Love

CPSIA information can be obtained
at www.ICGtesting.com
Printed in the USA
BVHW071339150719
553470BV00003B/316/P